Penny Ur's 77 Tips for Teaching Vocabulary

T0349545

Cambridge Handbooks for Language Teachers

This series, now with over 50 titles, offers practical ideas, techniques and activities for the teaching of English and other languages, providing inspiration for both teachers and trainers.

The Pocket Editions come in a handy, pocket-sized format and are crammed full of tips and ideas from experienced English language teaching professionals, to enrich your teaching practice.

Recent titles in this series:

Penny Ur's 77 Tips for Teaching Vocabulary

Penny Ur

Consultant and editor: Scott Thornbury

CAMBRIDGE
UNIVERSITY PRESS

CAMBRIDGE
UNIVERSITY PRESS

University Printing House, Cambridge CB2 8BS, United Kingdom

One Liberty Plaza, 20th Floor, New York, NY 10006, USA

477 Williamstown Road, Port Melbourne, VIC 3207, Australia

314–321, 3rd Floor, Plot 3, Splendor Forum, Jasola District Centre,
New Delhi – 110025, India

103 Penang Road, #05–06/07, Visioncrest Commercial, Singapore 238467

Cambridge University Press is part of the University of Cambridge.

It furthers the University's mission by disseminating knowledge in the pursuit of
education, learning and research at the highest international levels of excellence.

www.cambridge.org
Information on this title: www.cambridge.org/9781009074001

© Cambridge University Press 2022

First published 2022

20 19 18 17 16 15 14 13 12 11 10 9 8 7 6 5 4

Printed in Great Britain by CPI Group (UK) Ltd, Croydon CR0 4YY

A catalogue record for this publication is available from the British Library

ISBN 978-1-009-07400-1 Paperback
ISBN 978-1-009-07401-8 eBook

Contents

Read this first

The content and aims of this book

This book consists of a series of practical tips on vocabulary teaching. Their goal is to help the reader/teacher in a variety of teaching situations to decide which vocabulary items (both single words and phrases) to teach and how, and which kinds of learning and teaching strategies are likely to work well – or not so well. Most of them apply to the teaching of any language; a few are specific to English. The tips are based primarily on my own teaching experience, but in some cases are supported by ideas I've got from other teachers or the professional literature, or by insights from applied linguistics research.

Of course, any particular tip may work for me but not for you: we each have our own teaching personality and preferences and our situations and learner populations vary widely. Please relate to the tips cautiously, as recommendations from a colleague rather than as directives from an authority, and adopt, reject or adapt them according to your own professional judgement.

Types of tips

Most of the tips recommend practical procedures or strategies that can promote good learning of vocabulary. A few, however, are caveats: suggestions to avoid teaching procedures which may not lead to good learning, in spite of the fact that many teachers and textbooks use them (e.g., 'Avoid meaningless copying or repetition of the new items'). Some of the tips are generic practical principles, like 'Practise a lot' or 'Teach new vocabulary both in context and in isolation'; others are ideas for specific learner tasks or teacher strategies, like 'Use *yes/no* worksheets', or 'Use pictures and realia'.

Using this book

Teachers: The book is not intended to be read through page by page. Have a look at the Contents, see which sections or individual tips interest you and turn to them first. Or flip through the book, skipping the tips that don't seem relevant to your own teaching and focusing on those that are likely to be more helpful for you. Or if you are looking for a particular topic, use the Contents or Index to find it.

Teacher trainers/educators: Some of the tips in this book can be used as a starting point to provide student teachers with more substantial input on key research-based information: the use of corpora to establish frequency, for example (see Tip 44), or types, function and importance of **multi-word items** (**chunks**) (see Tip 4). Others can lead in to debates on more controversial subjects, such as the place of **L1** and translation (see Tips 27, 56) or the usefulness of **inferencing** (see Tip 49).

Materials writers: Many of the tips have immediate relevance for the design of coursebook components that deal with the teaching of vocabulary: in particular, those that deal with vocabulary selection and the design of enrichment and review procedures.

Added features

Research evidence: Many of the tips have footnotes citing research studies that support or give more information on suggestions made in the tips. A full list of these is shown on page 88.

Further recommended reading: A list of books and articles, grouped under topic headings, provides further information on some of the issues mentioned in the tips.

Glossary: A brief glossary explains terms that may not be familiar to the reader. Words appearing in the glossary are shown in **bold** in the text.

A: The importance of vocabulary learning

Vocabulary is the most important component of language to learn. You can communicate with limited grammar and less-than-accurate pronunciation, but you cannot do so without a lot of vocabulary. The more vocabulary a learner knows, the better they are likely to function in the new language.

---

1 Devote time to vocabulary teaching
2 Raise learners' awareness of the importance of vocabulary

---

1 Devote time to vocabulary teaching

> If learners have little or no exposure to the target language outside of class, they are not likely to pick up a lot of vocabulary just through reading and listening. It is therefore essential to devote time to deliberate vocabulary teaching in class.

A learner needs to know an enormous amount of vocabulary: at least five thousand words in order to cope with the needs of most communicative situations; much more if they wish to understand unsimplified texts and interact successfully in high-level discussions.

When learning our mother tongue, we acquired an extensive vocabulary incidentally: through listening and, more importantly, reading. But learners of a new language, particularly if they are learning in a country where the **target language** is not spoken outside the classroom, cannot do the same: their reading and listening outside class is likely to be in their mother tongue, and the limited amount of reading they will do in the new language, though important as a supplement (see Tip 73), is not enough to ensure they acquire the numbers of vocabulary items mentioned above.

We therefore need to spend instructional time on the deliberate presentation, explanation and review of new vocabulary: I would suggest at least a quarter of lesson time, and the same proportion of homework.

This does not, of course, mean simply taking a list of words and teaching them drily one by one! But it does mean:

- Drawing attention to the forms and meanings of new items encountered in texts (see Tips 43–49);
- Encouraging learners to write down new items and review them (see Tip 22);
- Introducing occasional new items for the sake of vocabulary enrichment (see Tip 52);
- Doing frequent vocabulary-review activities (see Tips 34–42);
- Including vocabulary tests in any periodic assessment procedures used during the course (see Tip 67).

Raise learners' awareness of the importance of vocabulary

> If learners are aware of the importance of vocabulary, they are more likely to be willing to put in the necessary effort to acquire it.

It's worth devoting some lesson time early in the course to awareness-raising discussions, with the aim of getting the students to appreciate why it is so important to learn a lot of vocabulary in the **target language**. If they are not very advanced, then do this in their mother tongue (assuming they all speak the same language, which you also know). Such awareness-raising is useful for various reasons.

First, it's a good idea for teachers of any subject to share with learners their reasons for teaching the way they do. Learners need to feel they are active partners in the learning process, that they know what is going on and why they are being asked to do certain things.

Second, it cannot be taken for granted that learners will know intuitively that vocabulary is important: not even all teachers are aware of its crucial role in the achievement of proficiency. (It's far more important than correct grammar!) If learners understand why and how all this vocabulary-focused activity will promote their success in learning, they are more likely to invest effort in doing it.

Third, once we move beyond the fairly basic levels of the target language (A1/A2), learners will need to supplement the vocabulary they are learning in class with active learning outside it (see Tip 73). We need, of course, to teach as much as we can in class (see Tip 1), but in most courses the number of teaching hours is too small to ensure enough vocabulary coverage. Successful learning of new vocabulary outside the classroom depends crucially on motivation: and motivation in its turn depends on an awareness of the importance of such learning.

B: Selecting vocabulary to teach

If you are using a coursebook, this will often give you guidance as to which vocabulary items to teach, though you may find that you want to omit some and add others. If you are choosing your own materials as you go, then the choice of which vocabulary items to teach will be completely up to you. In either case, the tips in this section may help you decide which to prioritise.

3 Prioritise the most common vocabulary items
4 Include multi-word items
5 Teach word families selectively
6 Teach occasional idioms and proverbs
7 Teach basic texting vocabulary
8 Use published vocabulary lists with caution
9 Prioritise internationally acceptable items
10 Avoid introducing lists of words that are all 'the same kind of thing'
11 Teach useful classroom vocabulary early on

Prioritise the most common vocabulary items

> **Learners need to acquire a lot of vocabulary, and the number of hours we have to teach it is limited. We therefore should not waste time teaching rare words that will not be very useful.**

Particularly in the case of elementary learners, our priority is to get them to master the most common vocabulary items, in order for them to feel as soon as possible that they are able to understand and convey basic messages in the new language.

Many elementary coursebook units focus on sets of words like colours or parts of the body (see Tip 10), with the result that learners are taught relatively rare words like *purple, toes,* before they know common and essential ones like *just, thing,* and may not learn useful multi-word **chunks** like *of course, go on.*

Often your own common sense will tell you which items from the materials are likely to be more common and useful. If you want more objective criteria, refer to a **corpus** (a large database of naturally occurring written and spoken texts in a specified language). See, for example, corpora listed on the Brigham Young University site (englishcorpora.org), or the sources referred to in Tip 44, which can tell you how frequent any particular vocabulary item is. As a rough guide: words that occur within the top 1,000 most frequent words are probably appropriate for beginners, or A1 learners; those within the 3,000 most frequent would be appropriate for learners up to about B1.

I'm not suggesting, of course, that *all* the vocabulary taught at early levels needs to be taken from the lists of the most frequent items: items that are essential for the theme or situation being taught or for understanding a text, or ones we need for classroom interactions or that are relevant to the learners' culture – all these will necessarily be included in any interesting language-teaching programme. But we should not spend too much time on them; the common, useful items need to be prioritised.

4   Include multi-word items

> **Vocabulary is not just single words. It also includes items which are composed of more than one word, but convey a single meaning like a word does. Some examples are *by the way, more or less, look after*.**

It has been estimated that at least one-tenth of the vocabulary we need to learn consists of **chunks** like these.

In many cases, these are *non-compositional*: that is, their meaning cannot be guessed by knowing the meaning of the component words and the grammar that links them. For example, you could not guess the meaning of *by and large* by putting together the basic meanings of *by, and,* and *large*. Very often such items can be paraphrased by single words: *by and large*, for instance, means the same as *generally*.

Even **compositional** chunks are worth teaching. First, even if it is clear what the item means, learners need to know, for their own production, that this is how the idea is idiomatically expressed in the **target language**. For example, 'What's the time?' in English is the conventional way of asking about the time of day, rather than the equivalent of 'How late is it?' as in German, or 'What hour is it?' as in Spanish. Second, memorising a common **multi-word item** can help fluency: the learner doesn't have to compose the phrase or sentence word by word, but can say the whole sequence straight off, confident that it is correct.

When choosing which vocabulary items to teach from a text, it is important to search for and identify chunks that occur within the text that it might be useful to draw students' attention to; your coursebook may not identify them (see Tip 45).

A useful list of the most frequent non-compositional chunks can be found in Martinez and Schmitt (2012) (see the full reference below).

Schmitt, N. and Martinez, R. (2012). 'A phrasal expressions list.' *Applied Linguistics*, 33(2), 299–320.

Teach word families selectively

> It is sometimes taken for granted that it is useful to teach word families: to add other items from the same family when teaching any new word. For example, together with *act* we might teach *acting, acted, activity, action, inactive*.

Note that not all words learnt earlier are necessarily the most basic form of the word: learners are likely to learn *computer* before *compute*, for example. So teaching another member of the **word family** may in fact mean teaching a base form when learners have just learnt a **derivative** rather than vice versa.

Other words from the same word family may not necessarily involve a **prefix** or **suffix**. The new family member may look and sound exactly the same as the basic word you have just taught – but be used as another **part of speech**. For example, in English, when teaching *sign* the noun, we may teach that the same word can also be a verb.

Teaching word families is, in principle, a quick and easy way of expanding vocabulary based on words the learners already know. But we need to be cautious: not all the family members of a given word are necessarily useful to the learner or easy to learn.

- Some derivatives have little or nothing to do with the root meaning of the word: a nuclear *reactor* for example has no obvious connection with the word *react*, or with the prefix *re-* or root verb *act*.
- Some members of a word family may be rare and not very useful to most classes: if you teach *proportion*, it is probably not a good idea to also teach *disproportionately*.

Bottom line: if you are going to teach other members from the same family as a new word, then focus on the most common and useful ones, with clear links to the meaning of the original word. Don't feel you need to try to teach them all.

6 Teach occasional idioms and proverbs

> There is a common belief that idioms (like *the best of both worlds* in English) are a common feature of the speech of native speakers – and that it is important to teach them. Neither of these ideas is true.

Idioms like *the best of both worlds* are very rare. This one, for example, occurs on average a little less than once per million words: about the same frequency as words like *scrutinise* or *evasive*, which we certainly would not see as useful items for any but the most academic level classes.

The same goes for proverbs: even an apparently common proverb like *better late than never* rates only 0.5 per million in frequency.

So why teach them?

- Because they happen to come up. If I find myself using an idiomatic expression like this, or encounter it in a text, then I'll teach it as extra enrichment.
- Because they are fun. Learners may enjoy learning the sometimes interesting, humorous or piquant idiomatic expressions that occur in another language.
- Because they may have cultural value. It is interesting to compare a proverb in the **target language,** with parallel, or contrasting proverbs in the **L1,** and explore the cultural implications.

Bottom line: I would not recommend teaching a whole set of idioms or proverbs for their own sake as part of the vocabulary syllabus, unless your class is very advanced (C1–C2). They are not common or useful enough to merit the time and effort needed. But teach occasional examples, for one or more of the reasons given above.

P.S. If you do teach an idiom, don't use pictures of the literal meaning (as opposed to the actual message) of the expression to teach it: for example, don't use a picture of someone pulling a leg to teach *to pull someone's leg*. If you want to use a picture, then use one that illustrates the communicative meaning.

Teach basic texting vocabulary

> The language of phone texting, using messaging apps, has developed as a genre in its own right, and has been extensively studied. Should 'texting' vocabulary therefore be part of the syllabus of a language course?

Some teachers would answer 'no' to this question: the language used in texting, some say, is an inferior shorthand, impoverishing rather than enriching language knowledge. Anyway, if learners need it, they will pick it up through exchanges with friends, they don't need us to teach it. And they might start using such language in formal writing, where it is unacceptable.

On the other hand, it is undeniable that our learners today will need to be able to communicate effectively through texting in their new language as much as – maybe more than – they will need to be able to compose and understand emails. If this is so, then surely we should be supporting their learning of the vocabulary for such communication. Also, there's the aspect of our credibility as teachers: we need to show that we are up to date with the development of the language and its use in modern genres.

In general, most of the vocabulary used in texting is similar to that of informal speech. Some differences specific to this genre are:

- Simplified spelling, (e.g., *nite* for *night*);
- Abbreviated or clipped words to save keying in long sequences of letters (e.g., *demo* for *demonstration*);
- Substitutions of single letters or symbols for full words (e.g., *u* for *you*, *4* for *for*);
- Initials (e.g., *asap, bfn*).

My own opinion is that there is a place for teaching such vocabulary, while making sure that our learners are aware that it is specific to texting and not appropriate for more formal writing. The selection of which items to teach is a more difficult issue: in general, choose the more common, well-established items that you use yourself, rather than very new ones that may not yet be widely recognised.

Use published vocabulary lists with caution

> Many teachers in recent years have begun to use published vocabulary lists as a basis for vocabulary selection. Such lists can be helpful, but should be used with caution.

Published vocabulary lists of the most common vocabulary items in English can be useful in designing or evaluating a vocabulary syllabus, or when deciding which theme-based items are most important to teach. Three major ones are the *General Service List* (GSL), the *Academic Word List* (AWL), and the *English Vocabulary Profile* (EVP).

Michael West's *General Service List*, originally published in 1953, is a list of 2,000 useful words, which is somewhat outdated, yet still surprisingly popular today. It has more recently been updated to the *New General Service List*, based on **corpus** data, of nearly 3,000 words, listed by frequency (http://www.newgeneralservicelist.org/).

The *Academic Word List* (https://www.wgtn.ac.nz/lals/resources/academicwordlist/information) includes 570 word families based on a corpus of academic texts from different disciplines. It is widely used in courses for university students whose mother tongue is not English studying in an English-medium university.

The *English Vocabulary Profile* (https://www.englishprofile.org/wordlists/evp), based primarily on a corpus of learner language and textbooks, includes both single words and **multi-word items**. You can type in any word or phrase and the EVP will tell you what level the item is according to the **CEFR** categories (A1, A2, B1, B2, C1, C2).

You will find other lists on the internet, too many to detail here. They vary quite widely in their content, according to the corpora they use and the criteria for inclusion adopted by compilers. Many do not distinguish between different meanings or parts of speech (e.g., *mean* may be listed as a single item); the majority only give single words and provide no information on frequency of multi-word items. You will, therefore, often need to use your own professional judgement in evaluating and supplementing information they provide (see Tip 44).

Teachers of English used to wonder whether to teach British or American vocabulary. Today this is an irrelevant question: the criterion for selection is rather whether the vocabulary item will be understood by people using English for international communication.

English is being taught these days primarily as a **lingua franca**, enabling communication between people speaking different languages. Only a minority of learners are planning to live, study or work in an English-speaking country. Most of us are therefore aiming to equip our students with the English that will be optimally useful to them internationally.

Most English vocabulary is internationally acceptable anyway: the common words and expressions that we teach in beginner or lower-intermediate classes are likely to be used in the same way anywhere English is spoken. However, at more advanced levels, we begin to encounter words where this is not true. The word *fortnight* is not comprehensible to most people who are not speakers of British English; *billfold* is confined to those speaking American English; and *prepone* (the opposite of *postpone*) to English speakers from India and Pakistan.

Teachers coming from English-speaking countries may not know – as I did not when I began teaching – which words and expressions commonly used in their native variety of the language are not internationally comprehensible. As time goes on, both teachers and materials writers are becoming increasingly aware of this issue and try to avoid teaching vocabulary that is limited to a particular speech community. Very often dictionaries can help: a good dictionary will tag a usage if it is limited (for example, *Br.E*, if it is used mainly, or only, in British English). I have yet to find, however, a dictionary which tells you which usage is most used internationally. A useful tool is the Glowbe **corpus** (https://www.english-corpora.org/glowbe/) which will show you, for any particular word or expression, whether its use is spread over a wide range of speech communities, or confined to only a few of them.

10 Avoid introducing sets of words that are all 'the same kind of thing'

> In many coursebooks for young beginners, new vocabulary is presented in lexical sets: for example, colours or animals. This probably does not facilitate learning.

There has been substantial research on whether it is a good idea to introduce new words in **lexical sets**. A number of studies have found that learners remembered sets of new items better if they were all different kinds of things (see the references below) than if they were from a list of words relating to the same **semantic field** and all the same **part of speech** (parts of the body, for example). It seems that if items have similar meanings the learner tends to confuse them, which slows down learning.

It seems likely that the same applies to the initial teaching of any sets of words that are 'the same kind of thing'. It is probably not a good idea to introduce together words pronounced similarly, or sets of **synonyms**, or items with similar grammatical structure (a list of phrasal verbs based on *get*, for example).

New words are likely to be learnt better if they are connected thematically or syntactically: if they tend to appear together in a particular kind of context or sentence. So, for example, it is better to teach *blue* with *sky* than *blue* with *red, yellow, green*.

Note that this applies only to the first time new vocabulary is presented. Single items taught later can be linked to sets of words already learnt (see Tip 25); and there are excellent review tasks that are based on grouping vocabulary items into sets: 'odd one out' exercises, for example, or brainstorming associations.

Erten, I. H. and Tekin, M. (2008). 'Effects on vocabulary acquisition of presenting new words in semantic sets versus semantically unrelated sets.' *System* 36 (3), 407–422.

Papathanasiou, E. (2009). 'An investigation of two ways of presenting vocabulary.' *ELT Journal* 63(4), 313–322.

Tinkham, T. (1997). 'The effects of semantic and thematic clustering in the learning of second language vocabulary.' *Second Language Research* 13(2), 138–63.

Teach useful classroom vocabulary
early on

In order to be able to run the lesson in the target language, it's essential to teach words and phrases that will be often used in lessons.

Inevitably, in many monolingual classes a lot of the instructions for how to do tasks and explanations of language points in beginner classes will be done in the learners' mother tongue (**L1**). But to use L1 to express things or activities that regularly come up in the classroom process is surely a lost opportunity for learning. Many kinds of words, phrases and even sentences are repeatedly used in lessons; once the learners have been taught them, they are likely to encounter them again and again and learn them well.

These include, of course, single words like *page, book, look, listen, read, word*. But perhaps even more important are standard teacher instructions like 'Please sit down', or 'Open your books at page …', as well as questions like 'Do you understand?', or evaluative comments like 'Excellent!' or 'Very good'. And scarcely less important are useful phrases for the learners themselves to memorise and use: 'I don't understand', 'Can you repeat that, please?'. Later, it is useful to teach standard coursebook instructions such as 'Circle the right answer' or 'Complete the sentence'. More advanced classes will need the words we use to talk about texts or the learning process: *paragraph, presentation, scan*. Other useful items these days relate to learning online: *chat box*, 'Mute/Unmute your microphone.'

If you are teaching face to face, it is useful to keep such items displayed in the classroom and add to the display as you teach more.

Once your students have a vocabulary of useful classroom language, don't let yourself lapse into using L1 for things they already know in the **target language,** or allow them to do the same (easier said than done, I know, but still …!).

C: Introducing new vocabulary

The goal of the first introduction of a new word or phrase is primarily to make learners aware of its form and meaning, and to do this clearly and with maximum impact. I'll go more deeply into ways of explaining meanings in the next section: this one gives some general tips on managing the first encounter with new vocabulary items.

12 Teach written and spoken forms together
13 Keep metalanguage (e.g., *adjective*) to a minimum
14 Teach first the most common form of a word
15 Teach one meaning at a time
16 Teach collocations (links with other words)
17 Teach how new words behave grammatically
18 Teach new vocabulary both in context and in isolation
19 Draw attention to problematic pronunciation
20 Draw attention to problematic spelling
21 Write up new vocabulary on the board and leave it there
22 Make sure learners write down new items
23 Make learners aware of common mistakes associated with a new item

In general, it helps if you make sure that learners encounter both how the new vocabulary item sounds and what it looks like when written. It's not so good to present the oral version first and delay teaching the spelling until later.

There are, of course, exceptions to this: if, for example, the students you are working with are not yet literate; or if they are in the early stages of learning a new language which uses a different writing system, when they obviously cannot yet decode the letters that form the word. But in most cases, seeing the written form will help learners perceive the spoken form more accurately, and vice versa. It will also help the item make more initial impact and leave a better memory trace which can be reinforced in later review (see Tips 34–42).

Some have claimed that presenting a word visually helps 'visual' learners, and presenting its written form is better for 'auditory' ones. However, I am sceptical about this: there is no research that I am aware of that supports this division, and in my experience most learners benefit from both seeing and hearing any new language material.

Finally, providing only the written, or only the spoken, form of a new word or expression may create mistaken perceptions in the learners' minds which may persist: for example, they may mispronounce a word because they have only seen the written form, or misspell it because they have only heard it – mistakes which will need to be corrected later. I remember as a child mispronouncing 'misled' as /maɪzld/ because I had only been exposed to it in print – and being laughed at. In foreign language teaching it is a pity to allow situations like this to arise when they could have been prevented.

13 Keep metalanguage (e.g., *adjective*) to a minimum

> The use of terms like *adjective* and *definite article* doesn't contribute very much to learners' understanding and learning of new vocabulary: try to avoid using them.

If you have taught the word *red* and are satisfied that your students have understood its meaning, then it is unlikely that they will try to use it, or understand it, as a verb, noun or adverb. The same goes for any other vocabulary item. The **part of speech** is an integral part of the meaning of a word: if you know the meaning of a word, you will be implicitly aware of its part of speech. It is therefore unnecessary for learners to write the part of speech by each new item they write down: a note of its meaning is all that is needed (see Tip 22).

A further factor to be taken into account here is the infrequency of most metalinguistic terms. The word *adjective* for example, appears only in the sixth thousand of Nation's frequency list of word families, the *BNC/COCA headword list* (https://www.wgtn.ac.nz/lals/resources/paul-nations-resources/vocabulary-lists) – which would make it, in **CEFR** terms, at least C1 level. Such terms are therefore not a very useful addition to most learners' general communicative vocabulary knowledge. If you do feel you want to teach grammatical aspects of a new word, use simpler terms: 'more than one' instead of *plural,* 'the' instead of *definite article.*

Exceptions to all this are where the term is fairly simple anyway and represents a feature which it is important for learners to understand: *count* and *non-count* for example, for those learning English whose own language treats this distinction much less consistently (e.g., has only one word for *much* and *many*).

Note that although metalinguistic terminology, in my view, is to be avoided as far as possible at beginner and intermediate levels, it may be useful with advanced learners, who are likely to understand and benefit from more abstract explanations.

Teach first the most common form of a word

> Many common words have grammatical variants (irregular pasts of verbs, for example) or derivatives formed with prefixes and suffixes. In general, teach the most common one – which may not be the 'base' word.

This tip looks obvious. Of course we teach a word like *see* before we teach the past *saw* and a word like *act* before we teach *action*. And in most cases, this is how it works: the **base word** is the most common, and to be taught first.

The simple present tense of the verb is the most frequently used tense of most verbs, so it makes sense to teach the base form that this requires. Only for a very few verbs – such as *bleeding, chasing, starving* – is the progressive/continuous form more common; and only one verb that I have found (*said*) is used more commonly in the past.

However, sometimes the simplest base word form is not the most common. In such cases, it is the most frequent form that should take the priority in teaching, not the one that looks simpler.

One example of this is plurals such as *children, people* – much more common than *child, person*. Similarly, most parts of the body that occur in pairs are more frequently found in the plural: *eyes*, *ears* and *feet* are more common than *eye, ear, foot*. In such cases it makes sense to teach the plural first – it will probably be encountered first anyway – and come on to the singular later.

Another example is words with derivational **prefixes** and **suffixes**. It is sometimes assumed that learners will first learn the base form of a word and later its derivations. However, in many cases the base word is actually rarer than one or more of its derivations, so it is better to teach the derivation first. Some examples are *government, beautiful, accessible*, where the base forms *govern, beauty, access* are less common.

15 Teach one meaning at a time

> Many words have multiple meanings, so it is tempting to teach some or all of these when introducing the word. But it's usually best to teach only the most common one first.

A lot of the most common words in any language are *polysemes*: they have accumulated other meanings over time, mainly through metaphorical association: *head* as part of the body and *head* meaning the leader or principal of an organisation, for example. The question is whether to teach two or more of such meanings at first encounter, or only the meaning implied in the context where the word occurs.

Supposing, for example, you come across the word *crane* in English, meaning a machine used in building. Are you also going to teach that it is the name of a large migrating bird? If you encounter *star* meaning a twinkling light in the sky, are you going to teach that it also means an outstanding actor or singer?

In the first case, the answer is fairly clearly 'no', because the word *crane* meaning a kind of bird is rare and not particularly useful to most learners. The second meaning of *star*, on the other hand, is actually more common than the first, so the same reasoning would not work here; nevertheless, it is probably better to stay with the primary meaning as it appears in context, simply in order not to overload learners' memories with multiple meanings at first encounter.

Note that very often, as with both examples above, the most common meaning is not the original basic one, but a metaphorical extension. If we are not encountering the word in context, but simply teaching new words in isolation (see Tip 52), then we should teach the most common meaning first, not necessarily the original concrete one.

Teach collocations (links with other words)

> When you teach a new word, it makes sense to teach it together with the words it is likely to go with in a natural communicative context (collocation).

Many words tend to co-occur with other specific words in context: for example, a certain adjective will be followed by a certain preposition, even if there does not seem to be any particular logical reason for it based on meaning; or certain kinds of objects may follow certain verbs, and so on. Because the link is often apparently purely arbitrary it is useful to teach the **collocations** associated with a particular word when introducing the word itself.

For example, English says 'angry *with*' and not '*angry on*' as some other languages do; 'afraid *of*' rather than '*afraid from*'; 'responsibility *for*' rather than '*responsibility of*'. It therefore makes sense to teach, for example, the whole phrase *angry with* rather than just *angry*, and so on.

An associated problem is the choice between two apparently synonymous words, which differ mainly in their collocational links. Some verbs, for example, are differentiated mainly by the objects they **collocate** with rather than their basic meaning. An example in English is the distinction between *make* and *do*: you 'make an effort', for instance, but 'do your homework'. Similarly, some apparently synonymous adjectives tend to collocate with different nouns: *high* and *tall*, for example, or *big* and *large*, *small* and *little*. There are some cases where these are interchangeable, but many where they are not: it would sound odd to refer to a '*high person*' or a '*tall mountain*', '*a large difference*', or '*a little amount*'. In such cases, it helps to explain 'the kind of thing' that each collocates with, and also to provide plenty of examples of the most common combinations.

17 Teach how new words behave grammatically

> This tip looks at a variety of grammatical aspects relating to specific words, or kinds of words, which it is useful to teach learners when introducing the new item.

This is important particularly where the equivalent word in the learners' L1 has a different grammar, which might lead learners to make errors. When we are teaching common modal verbs like *can, should, must,* for instance, in English, it is useful to draw learners' attention to the fact that they take a simple infinitive after them, without *to*, since many other languages may use the equivalent of *to*. Some English verbs, like *enjoy* and *hate,* take *-ing*, and have parallel verbs in other languages which may use the equivalent of *to*. Such points taught at first encounter with the new verb can help learners avoid errors later (see Tip 23).

Similarly, it is useful when teaching some English non-count nouns to tell learners that they cannot appear in the plural. This is not necessary where the noun is clearly something that is unlikely to have a plural anyway, like *sugar*, for example, or *wisdom*. But other words are more tricky: common learner errors are forms like **researches*, **advices*, or **informations*, because these words can occur in the plural in the learners' L1.

Another area where initial teaching of a word can help learners avoid grammatical errors is the use of definite/indefinite articles, which may behave differently in the learners' L1. An example is abstract or general terms: English refers to *happiness* or *music* with no definite article, but these words translate into other languages preceded by the definite article: *la felicidad* (Spanish) or *la musique* (French). Similarly, there is the use of *a* with a profession: I would say of myself in English, 'I am a teacher,' but some other languages omit the article when expressing the same idea.

Teach new vocabulary both in context and in isolation

> Teachers are often urged to teach vocabulary in the context of a sentence or full text; but it is also useful to look at the new item in isolation, particularly when it is being taught for the first time.

When a learner encounters a new item in the context of a spoken text, it may be difficult to identify it as a separate word or phrase because of the unclear borders between words in the stream of speech. We need, therefore, to identify it and focus on it in isolation, temporarily, to make sure it is perceived accurately.

Another reason for teaching or learning an item in isolation is the factor of use of time: it takes a lot longer to relate to each item within a full-sentence context than it does to do so on its own. For example, learners are sometimes told to write the new items in their notebooks together with examples of the item in a sentence context. But it takes time for them to write sentences, especially if they have to compose them themselves, and it is questionable whether all this writing is in fact worth the time and effort in terms of learning benefits.

Similarly, we often want to remind our students of the new vocabulary items at the end of the lesson in order to help them to remember them. In such cases, we don't really have time to contextualise each within a sentence. It makes more sense to have a quick review of only the target items themselves: perhaps by challenging learners to recall them or translate them. Later review will, of course, also include activities that engage with the target items in context (see, for example, Tip 59).

A useful occasional compromise is to insert items in 'mini-contexts': two- or three-word phrases that contextualise a new item: adding an appropriate adjective to a newly-learnt noun, for example.

19 Draw attention to problematic pronunciation

> When learners encounter a new word within a reading text, they may not be aware of how it is pronounced, and may mispronounce it when using it themselves, even if they know the meaning.

There are two main sources of the pronunciation problems that learners encounter when learning a new word. One is when the spelling does not clearly correspond with its pronunciation. The second is the pronunciation of sounds that may not exist in the learners' L1, and may be difficult for them to hear, let alone articulate themselves.

The problem of spelling is particularly acute for those learning English as an additional language, owing to the fact that a single sound in that language may be represented in writing by a variety of letters or letter-combinations, and vice versa (see Tip 20).

With regard to difficulty of articulation: a new word may be misheard or mispronounced owing to the sheer unfamiliarity of a new sound – for example, the guttural 'ayin' for English speakers learning Arabic. Alternatively, the sound may be close to one in the learners' L1, and they may be unable to perceive that it is in fact different: Arabic speakers, for example, tend to substitute the familiar /b/ sound for the English /p/. In both such cases, mispronunciation may lead to misunderstanding. So, it is a good idea when introducing a new word which includes such sounds to draw learners' attention to the pronunciation and get them to practise articulating the word themselves.

Note that the neutral vowel sound or 'schwa' (/ə/) used in unstressed syllables in English, in words such as *away* or *together*, may also be taught when introducing a new word that exemplifies it: but it is arguably less important to teach than the examples above, since pronouncing the vowel giving its full value is unlikely to lead to misunderstanding.

> The teaching of a new word normally involves teaching its spelling, and is an opportunity to raise awareness of spelling conventions. There is also evidence that awareness of the spelling of a new word helps learners remember it.

This tip relates mainly to English, in which there is not always a predictable and consistent correspondence between sounds and letters. The spelling of some English words seems to be completely arbitrary (*what, one, busy*, for example), and these need to be taught and practised one by one, as the new words are encountered. Such words are almost all relatively common and typically acquired by learners at an elementary level.

The vast majority of English words, however, though not displaying regular and transparent correspondence between individual letters and sounds, do conform to regular spelling conventions. There are common combinations of letters that have consistent pronunciation (e.g., **bigrams** like *th, ee* and **suffixes** like *-tion*). There are rules like the 'magic e' (an 'e' after a single consonant at the end of a word causes the preceding vowel to be pronounced like its name as in *nine, inflate*). For some other useful rules see Tip 77.

Another aspect of the spelling of individual words in English is the use of upper-case letters and punctuation in names and abbreviations: the capitalisation of the first letter of a proper noun, for example. Abbreviations expressed as initials are almost always written in upper-case letters, but have mostly dropped the full stops after each letter, so teach *UN, BBC* rather than *U.N.* or *B.B.C.* Research indicates that drawing learners' attention to the written form of a new word and associated spelling rules may well improve overall retention of the new item (see the reference below).

Krepel, A., de Bree, E. H. and de Jong, P. F. (2021). 'Does the availability of orthography support L2 word learning?' *Reading and Writing*, 34(2), 467–496.

21 Write up new vocabulary on the board and leave it there

Anything we can do to reinforce learning of a new item is good! Leaving the new items written up on the board after teaching them is a simple initial step towards such reinforcement.

Teaching the written form of an item implies writing it up on the board: it is not enough just to draw learners' attention to it in their textbooks. The actual movement involved in the creation of the written image on the board (whether you are writing manually or typing) draws attention: as does its relatively large size and the possibility of using colour.

If, however, you then delete the new vocabulary in order to make room for whatever is coming next, you convey the message 'this doesn't matter any more'. You also deny students the possibility of looking again at the new vocabulary during the lesson. If you need space, then contract the new vocabulary display slightly and move it aside (if you are using a digital display); or delete it and rewrite it at the side (if you have a conventional white- or black-board).

If you teach more vocabulary later in the lesson, add the new items to the previous list, so that by the end of the lesson all the new vocabulary learnt in this lesson is there ready for you to note down for future reference.

Leaving the vocabulary on the board also furnishes the basis for a quick review or reminder later in the lesson. For example, you might elicit translation of each of the items; or tell students to close their eyes, delete an item and challenge them to identify which is missing; or give them a few seconds to look through the vocabulary again, then delete it and challenge them to recall the entire list.

Make sure learners write down new items

> When learners write down new items, this achieves two learning goals: first, the actual writing directs learners' attention to the item; second, it creates a record they can refer to when reviewing later.

The attention paid to the act of writing helps learning, provided that this implies awareness of both form and meaning: just mechanically writing down something, however many times you do it, does not help very much. So it makes sense to require your students to note down not only the item itself, but also a reminder of what it means – which they can do however they like, as long as it is clear to them. In the majority of cases, this will be a translation into their **L1**. Alternatives are drawings, brief explanations, or samples of use in phrases that make the meaning clear. They don't have to add **phonemic transcriptions**, or the **part of speech** or other members of the same **word family**. Similarly, adding full sentences contextualising the new item is time consuming, not to say tedious, and does not contribute much to learning.

How should the items be ordered? Alphabetical order is not a good idea: it means constantly leafing or scrolling back and forth, and it is unlikely anyway that learners will need to look up the items later according to their first letter. It is probably best simply to note them down in the order in which they are learnt. Learners can later delete any items which they are sure they remember, thus keeping the list to a more manageable length.

Note that it is not essential for learners to keep separate vocabulary notebooks for this purpose: they can write the vocabulary into their digital devices, or in their regular course notebooks.

23 Make learners aware of common mistakes associated with a new item

> If learners are made aware in advance of problems that are likely to occur with specific vocabulary items, this will help them to avoid associated errors.

Experienced teachers are usually aware of the most common errors their students are likely to make in their speech or writing in the **target language**. Many of these are associated with **L1 interference**: learners tend to carry over assumptions from their **L1** and apply them, often mistakenly, to the new language.

Where we know in advance that a certain error is very likely with a new vocabulary item, it is a good idea to draw learners' attention to it, rather than waiting for them to make a mistake and be corrected. Such awareness-raising may prevent the error being made at all; but even if an individual learner forgets, makes the error and needs to be corrected, the fact that they have been told about the problem previously will help them understand and take on board the correction.

Key areas of learner error are grammar, pronunciation and spelling: see Tips 17, 19, 20 for examples of features in these areas which it is worth drawing learners' attention to at first encounter with new vocabulary items.

The same principle applies to aspects of meaning of new vocabulary. For example, if we know that English only uses the one word *wear* to relate to a wide range of items of clothing, we need to point this out when teaching it to learners whose L1 employs different verbs with different garments. Another feature to look out for is **false friends**: *sympathetic* in English does not mean the same as very similar-looking and -sounding words in some other languages, and it is worth emphasising this when we first teach the word.

D: Clarifying meanings of new vocabulary

There are lots of different ways of explaining the meaning of a new word or expression. In this section I'll look at a range of strategies, and discuss where and why they are more or less effective, and how they can be combined for optimal learning.

24 Explain meanings yourself, rather than sending learners to a dictionary

In a lesson where you are available to provide information, it is time-saving and more helpful to learners if you explain meanings of new words yourself.

The dictionary is, of course, a valuable tool for vocabulary learning, and I am not suggesting learners should not use it. But if the goal is to get your students to understand the meaning of a new vocabulary item during a lesson, rather than the use of the dictionary for its own sake, then it is better to explain it yourself.

First, looking up words in the dictionary takes more time: even with digital dictionaries the learner has to type in the word (accurately!), and with print ones they have to leaf through to find the word. Second, even when they find the word, there may be problems (in a monolingual dictionary) of understanding the definition, or, when there are several possibilities, of choosing the right one. Third, there is the problem of **multi-word items** like *as though* or *a great deal*: the learner may not realise that they need in fact to look for a meaning of a combination of words rather than just one of them, and even if they do, it may not be clear under what headword (in a print dictionary) this should be searched for.

Your own explanation will be expressed in language appropriate to your students: their **L1** or simplified **target language**. You will also know in advance which meaning of a word is needed in any particular case.

The use of dictionaries for learners in lesson time should be in general limited to those activities which are deliberately designed to teach dictionary skills (see Tip 75). Outside actual lessons, learners will mostly use them when they need to understand a difficult word in a written text on their own without any knowledgeable speaker of the target language to help them.

Link the new vocabulary to items previously taught

> Building on previous knowledge when teaching something new is a basic principle of good teaching of any subject. In vocabulary teaching, this means linking the new item with ones the learners already know.

We may explain the meaning of a new word in various ways (see, for example, Tips 27–29); but one useful strategy is to use previously learnt words as a 'hook' to clarify meaning: *miserable* means the same as *very sad*; *rise* is the opposite of *fall*; a *lion* is a kind of *animal*, from the *cat family*.

After the initial explanation, learners can be asked to brainstorm other words or expressions that are associated with the new word: what other animals have we learnt, other than *lion*? What other negative feelings can you think of besides *miserable*? Or more general associations: what other words does the word *rise* remind you of?

Another possibility is to link the new words with others it might 'go with' in a phrase – it doesn't have to be a complete sentence. For example, how might you describe a lion? ('a big lion', 'an African lion' …); or where might you find a lion? ('a lion in a tree', 'a lion in a safari park' …); or what can – or can't – a lion do? ('A lion can run', 'A lion can't read' …).

At a more advanced level, you can explore with learners the differences between the new word and a previously-learnt one with a similar meaning: what are the differences, for example, between *miserable* and *sad*? (See Tip 31.)

Such processes not only reinforce the learning of the new item, and the way it can be used within mini-contexts, they also help to integrate it within the network of language items – grammatical or lexical – that students have already learnt. In addition, they obviously provide opportunities to review a range of other words and expressions.

26 Explain meanings briefly

> For good learning of a new item to take place, we
> need to make sure that learners' initial perception and
> understanding is established as quickly as possible, to free
> up more time for review and consolidation of learning.

One of the problems of teaching the vocabulary of a new language in a
formal course of study is that there isn't usually enough time to teach
all the vocabulary the learners need (see Tip 1). This not only means
that learners need to supplement their learning outside the classroom, it
also means that we need to use time as efficiently as possible in order to
ensure optimum learning outcomes from our lessons.

Extended explanations of a new word are used by teachers who feel
that they wish to avoid the use of **L1**, but can't find a quick **synonym**
or easy way to paraphrase the meaning. It is often quite difficult for
learners to understand such explanations; typically, they only begin to
get the point towards the end. But time spent 'not understanding' is
time wasted as far as vocabulary learning is concerned. They may be
getting some practice in listening to the **target language**, but they are not
learning the new word very efficiently.

It makes sense, therefore, to keep the explanation brief in order for
learners to understand what the new item means as soon as possible.
They will then have more time to engage with it to make and receive
messages that they understand, and thus begin to consolidate learning.

One implication of this recommendation is that giving explanations
of new vocabulary using the target language is often not very efficient.
Supplementing with pictures, mime, etc. may help; but in many cases it
makes sense simply to provide a quick translation into the learners' L1
(see Tip 27).

Use the learners' mother tongue (L1) to help clarify

> The use of the learners' L1 to clarify the meaning of a new item, in a class where the teacher knows the learners' language(s), not only saves time: it is also likely to be clearer and more learner-friendly.

It is gradually becoming more acceptable, worldwide, to use the learners' mother tongue in language teaching (see the reference below). In vocabulary teaching, translating a new word conveys its meaning rapidly and clearly; it takes maybe a second or two, as compared to a minute or more that a target-language explanation could take. Perhaps paradoxically, the use of the **L1** to explain vocabulary actually frees up more time for target-language use in providing examples, contexts and associations for the new item.

It is also more learner-friendly; many learners like the teacher to explain things in the L1, and feel 'safer' if they can relate the meaning of the new item to a word they know in their own language. Similarly, most learners of a second language prefer to use a bilingual rather than a monolingual dictionary to look up meanings.

A useful technique based on L1 is the 'keyword' method: in order to remember the meaning of a new word, the learner links it to an image that reminds him or her of a similar word in the L1. For example, in order for an English-speaking learner of Spanish to remember that the word *ropa* means 'clothes', they imagine a bundle of clothes tied up in a rope. You can suggest such associations when teaching the new word, or get students to think of their own.

Translating into the L1 is obviously more difficult to do in a multilingual classroom, or in one where the teacher does not know the learners' language. But even in such situations, the teacher can encourage learners who have understood a new word to help classmates from the same linguistic background by telling them the translation.

Kerr, P. (2014). *Translation and own-language activities*. Cambridge: Cambridge University Press.

28 Use pictures and realia

> The value of the use of pictures and realia (actual objects) to explain the meanings of new words lies mainly in the fact that such illustrations make more impact and are more motivating than dry explanations or translations.

Pictures and realia are traditionally used a lot in classes of (beginner) young learners: partly because it is assumed that young learners respond better to pictures than do older ones, and partly because the vocabulary taught at the elementary levels tends to be more concrete and easier to depict.

However, older learners also like and benefit from looking at pictures (otherwise, why would newspapers include illustrations?). And there is some evidence that pictures can help learners retain the meanings of abstract, as well as concrete words: for example, a picture of someone looking frightened can help a learner remember the word for 'fear' (see the reference below).

In my experience, realia make more impact than pictures, so use them whenever you can. There is no good reason for a teacher to explain, for example, what an apple is by showing a picture of it, when it is fairly easy to get hold of the object itself. Teachers who have small children can borrow their toys to teach things like vehicles, animals and so on.

The advantages of pictures and realia in providing interesting and motivating illustrations of the meanings of new vocabulary are undoubted. The only problem is that they are sometimes ambiguous: a picture of someone laughing to indicate 'happy' for example, might be interpreted as 'smile' or 'laugh' or even 'face'. However, if you back it up with a quick **L1** translation to accompany the target-language word, you will achieve both clarity and impact.

Farley, A. P., Ramonda, K. and Liu, X. (2012). 'The concreteness effect and the bilingual lexicon: The impact of visual stimuli attachment on meaning recall of abstract L2 words.' *Language Teaching Research*, 16(4), 449–466.

Use mime, gesture, facial expression

> Your own body is a vital visual aid. It can be used, often even more effectively than pictures or realia, to facilitate or reinforce learners' understanding of meaning and make impact.

One of the advantages of face-to-face teaching is that the teacher is able to take full advantage of facial expression and body movements to express meanings; and these often are more effective in drawing learners' attention than are static pictures or realia. And there is some research-based evidence that seeing the teacher acting out word meanings, or acting them out themselves, helps learners remember the target items better than just verbal clarifications (see the reference below).

There is a limit, of course, to the kinds of meaning that can be conveyed clearly and solely through physical movement. Obviously, you can indicate parts of the body; action verbs can be demonstrated through mime and gesture (*eat, walk, sit, point*) and moods and emotions through your expression (*happy, fear, angry*).

It is a mistake, however, to think that this kind of demonstration is the only way you can use movement and facial expression in teaching vocabulary. A more important, though less obvious, function is as a back-up to other means of explanation: to add clarity and impact. If you want to explain words like *unfortunately, boring, beautiful,* or **multi-word items** like *over there, I don't care,* you are likely to do so through a brief definition or translation: but your accompanying physical movement and facial expression will support the verbal explanation, and make the item and its meaning more interesting and memorable.

You don't have to be a talented actor to use mime, gesture and facial expression: but you need to be willing, perhaps, to move outside your 'comfort zone' in the way you allow your face and body to express things in the classroom.

Thornbury, S. (2013). The learning body. In Arnold, J. and Murphey, T. (Eds.), *Meaningful action: Earl Stevick's influence on language teaching* (pp. 62–78). Cambridge: Cambridge University Press.

30 Vary the way you explain

> There are a number of ways of conveying the meaning of new vocabulary to learners: it's important to be aware of the variety available, and not to get stuck in a rut of using only one or two routine methods.

The main methods that can be used to convey the meaning of new vocabulary are the following: definition in the **target language** ('*rich* means you have a lot of money'); quick definitions in the form of **synonyms** and opposites (*trot* is like *run*; *cheap* is the opposite of *expensive*); examples of the kinds of things included in the item (*swimming, football* and *tennis* are all *sports*); sentences using the item in context ('That video was very funny: it made me *laugh*.'); pictures and realia; mime and facial expression; translation.

It is unfortunately too easy to get into the habit of using, for example, only definitions, or only **L1** translations, for all new vocabulary.

One reason for varying your methods is simply for the sake of variation itself: as in many components of the teaching process, repeated routines tend to bore learners, and we can raise interest by using different methods at different times. Another is that any specific item is likely to be more, or less, amenable to certain types of clarifications: action verbs are probably best taught through mime, for example. For each item, we need in principle to select the method that is likely to convey the meaning most clearly, effectively and impactfully. Obviously, you won't have time and attention to be able to think about and select an appropriate method for every single new item you teach – but be aware of the basic principle, and apply it where you can.

It is good to combine two or more methods for any particular new item. For example, you might show a picture and back it up with a definition; you might provide a synonym and then add examples in context; you might demonstrate something, and then translate it to make sure the demonstration is clear.

Teach where it is appropriate/ inappropriate to use a new item

31

Knowing the meaning(s) of a word or expression will not always enable a learner to know when and where to use it in real-world communication. They also need to know in what contexts it may or may not be appropriate.

Most vocabulary we teach is neutral, in that it can be used in most contexts. However, some items are appropriate for some and not for others. The most common distinction of this kind is that between informal versus formal: usually informal conversation versus formal written prose. In English, items marked for informal usage include words like *guy, kid, lots of, a bit of* as compared to *person, child, much/many, a little.* As a rule, phrasal verbs are informal, whereas synonymous single-word verbs (often Latinate in origin) are formal: *set up* v *establish*, for example; or *put off* v *postpone*.

An interesting exception to the generalisation that informal language is mainly used in conversation is texting, in which informal language is written down. Learners need to know that many items appropriate for texting on their cellphones cannot be used in formal writing (shortened spellings, for example, like *nite, U*). Some vocabulary common in texting is unlikely to be used even in informal conversation (*LOL*, for example), and other items would be more likely to be pronounced as full words rather than initials or acronyms (*FAQ, bfn, asap*).

Some items are confined to certain contexts and might give offence or cause discomfort if used outside them. This clearly applies to 'taboo' items: oaths or words that relate to sexual activity or excretion (like *shit* in English). Less obvious are terms that are not so clearly taboo, but might embarrass or offend: for example, instead of referring to a child as 'a low-level learner' or, worse, 'backward', more neutral expressions should be used like, for example, 'non-academic' or 'with special needs'. In the same way, learners need to know to avoid explicitly gender-linked words and to prefer gender-neutral: *actor* rather than *actress*; *humanity* rather than *mankind*.

32 Teach connotations

> The meanings of some words include not only what they
> denote in the real world, but also underlying connotations:
> negative or positive associations, or connections with
> particular types of context.

If you look up *connotation* online, the main focus will be on 'positive/
negative' implications or positive/neutral/negative: typical examples in
English are *slim* v *skinny, famous* v *well-known* v *notorious*. These are
fairly clear examples, and a good dictionary will provide a clear positive
or negative connotation as part of their definition.

More tricky are the many words where the connotation may only
occasionally surface, and the word may in one context be used to express
a purely objective idea, and in another convey underlying disapproval:
for example, *politics, exploit, smell*. Commonly, the real-life, concrete
meaning of a word is neutral and only when used figuratively does the
word take on a negative or positive connotation: for example, *soft* as
in 'soft butter' v 'a soft voice' – in the latter example, *soft* has clearly
more positive connotations than *quiet*. Words that have to do with size
or height very often have positive/negative connotations: the positive
associated with the high, broad or large, negative with things that are
low, narrow or small (the word *great* for example, originally simply
'large in size' has come to mean 'very good', 'famous' or 'admirable').

The last-mentioned distinction is common to many languages and
therefore may not need much teaching; the connotations of others,
however, may be culture-specific, which is why you may need to teach
them as you teach the new word.

There are occasionally connotations other than positive/negative that
it may be useful to note when teaching new words to more advanced
learners: for example, the word *hurry* in English implies stress as well
as speed, whereas *rush* does not; *load* means a weight that is carried;
burden carries the connotation of the difficulty of carrying it.

Avoid asking learners to study corpus data themselves

> In the literature on data-driven learning, it is recommended that learners use corpora in order to check out how a vocabulary item is used. This, however, is time-consuming and rarely worth the effort.

It is useful – and sometimes fun! – for a teacher occasionally to check out a particular word or **multi-word item** on a **corpus** (a large database of written or spoken text in the **target language**) in order to find out how common it is, or whether it is more common in speech or writing, and so on. Whether it is useful for a learner to do the same is doubtful.

There have been a number of studies in recent years promoting data-driven learning (DDL) (see the reference below): the idea that the learners themselves should have access to primary data, as provided by a corpus, in order to learn about a vocabulary item. For example, they might use a corpus concordance to find out the **connotations** (see Tip 32) of a particular word. Most of the studies I have read find that learners can indeed gain knowledge about a new word from corpus study; but clearly this takes a good deal longer than looking it up in a dictionary. So it is probably not worth the effort.

This is even more true if the comparison is made not between corpus and dictionary, but between corpus and teacher. You, the teacher, can provide the relevant information in a fraction of the time it takes for the learner to look up a vocabulary item in the corpus; and if back-up information from a corpus is needed, your interpretation of the data is probably more reliable.

The exception to all this might be with very advanced academic learners who are likely to work faster and may find the search and discovery involved in corpus use interesting in itself as well as revealing.

Boulton, A. (2017). 'Corpora in language teaching and learning.' *Language Teaching*, 50(4), 483–506.

E: Vocabulary review and practice

It is essential to provide learners with plenty of opportunities to review new items through practice activities. This section provides some ideas on how to make vocabulary practice effective.

34 Practise a lot

35 Avoid meaningless copying or repetition of the new items

36 Give tasks that get learners to retrieve

37 Make exercises interesting to do

38 Personalize vocabulary review

39 Review after a time-gap

40 Try to avoid word games

41 Use collaborative activities

42 Encourage learners to use new vocabulary in their own speech and writing

> Research indicates that the more times a learner
> encounters a vocabulary item, the better they remember
> it (see the reference below); conversely, they are likely to
> forget one they encounter only once.

The exact number of times that a learner needs to re-encounter a new item in order to remember it permanently will vary, depending on various factors: how difficult the item is (form or meaning); the level and ability of the learner; the quality of the new encounter(s) (see Tip 36). A rough estimate is between six and 16.

Very common words are likely to be encountered several times without any particular focused practice: words like *open, sure,* for example. But as soon as you get on to less frequent items, even if they are not very advanced (*kitchen,* or *discover,* for example), the chances that the learner will come across them enough times by chance in a new text or interaction are low. Or by the time they do come across the second encounter they may have forgotten what they learnt from the first (see Tip 39 on spacing).

We therefore need to provide systematic, regular and focused vocabulary practice exercises in lessons (see Section H for some practical ideas). It might be expected that course materials should provide this practice; but most coursebooks I have used do not provide nearly enough. Clearly it is not going to be feasible within the lesson time at our disposal to provide six or more review exercises of every single new item we teach: but we can at least note them all down as we teach them, and make sure that we remind learners of them in class at least two or three times, run periodic tests, and include vocabulary review tasks as regular homework assignments.

Webb, S. (2007). 'The effects of repetition on vocabulary knowledge.' *Applied Linguistics,* 28(1), 46–65.

35 Avoid meaningless copying or repetition of the new items

Teachers have sometimes been urged to get their students to say new vocabulary repeatedly, or copy it in writing, over and over, in the hope that this will help them remember. It probably won't.

It is certainly useful to get learners to pronounce a new item themselves and write it down when learning it for the first time, in order to make sure they have perceived its spoken and written forms correctly, and to help them take it into short-term memory as the first stage in learning. It is also important to review new items in order to consolidate knowledge (see Tip 34). But meaningless repetitions will not aid such consolidation. There are various reasons for this.

First, mechanical repetition, whether orally or in writing, does not involve attention: you can do it without thinking. And in order for there to be learning, the material to be learnt needs to be noticed: research indicates that we actually retain little or nothing through 'subliminal' or unconscious learning (see the reference below). Second, part of that noticing needs to be directed towards meaning: just saying or writing an item involves only form. Third, it is boring: and we do not, on the whole, learn well when we are bored.

This is not to say that there is no place for learning by heart and repetition in vocabulary learning; but activities involving these need to require attention and be meaningful and interesting. Some examples are learning by heart and reciting rhymes, poems, chants or dialogues – or even longer chunks of text such as speeches or stories – that contextualise target vocabulary. Such activities need, however, to be carefully designed so that the learners performing such texts understand what they are saying and demonstrate this understanding through the way they say them.

Schmidt R. W. (1990). 'The role of consciousness in second language learning.' *Applied Linguistics*, 11(2), 129–58.

Give tasks that get learners to retrieve

> If learners make an effort to remember either the meaning or the form of the new vocabulary – and succeed – this is the best way to reinforce their learning of the item.

There is substantial research to indicate that **retrieval** of a new item from memory is far more effective in helping learners to remember it than is mere repetition or further incidental encounters in context (see the references below). This is not to say that just seeing or hearing the item again – provided that the learner understands its meaning – is useless: far from it! And it is certainly very quick and easy. But it is less effective than retrieval-based tasks for reinforcing memory.

Retrieval of meaning takes place if you provide the students with the target item and challenge them to demonstrate that they understand what it means. This could be through multiple-choice questions, or gap-fills with a word bank, or matching of item and definition, or simple translation into **L1**. More difficult, but perhaps more effective for learning, is retrieval of form, where you provide the meaning – through a definition, for example, or a picture, or the L1 equivalent – and ask the students to produce the target item themselves in response. The first involves **receptive knowledge**; the second, **productive**.

It is best to try to time such tasks so that the students can in fact succeed in retrieving; the best learning results from effortful recall. If they learnt an item too long ago, then they'll have forgotten it and will not be able to retrieve it: in which case you'll need to remind them and re-teach. Such processes are still valuable: in many cases the student hasn't remembered the item well enough to do the retrieval task but retains a vague impression of it, and your reminder will help them remember it for next time.

Karpicke, J. and Roediger, H. L. (2008). 'The critical importance of retrieval for learning.' *Science*, 319, 966–968.

Laufer, B. and Rozovski-Roitblat, B. (2011). 'Incidental vocabulary acquisition: the effects of task type, word occurrence and their combination.' *Language Teaching Research*, 15(4), 391–412.

37 Make exercises interesting to do

> Many coursebook or online exercises are boring – both for learners to do and for teachers to check. We can increase interest by using some simple 'tweaks' requiring little preparation.

Standard vocabulary exercises based on multiple-choice, sentence-completion/gap-fill or matching tend to be rather tedious to do – and to check. This is partly because they are based on one, predictable answer, partly because their content is unlikely to relate to topics of interest to the learners, partly because the challenge is only 'getting them all right' with no interesting task attached, and no flexibility as to how much to do or in what order.

Here are a few ideas to make exercises more interesting:

- Time-limit: tell students they can work in pairs or alone and have exactly three minutes to do as many of the items as they can. Give them a clear signal when to start and when to finish.
- Open-ending: in a 'gap-fill', after filling in gaps from a word bank, challenge students to find other words to fill the gaps; or other sentences to contextualise the words (for more on open-ending, see Tip 64).
- Recall: after you've finished an exercise, tell students to close their books and recall all the words that were practised in it, or as many of the actual sentences as they can remember (for more recall tasks see Tip 58).
- Personalize: tell students to re-word sentences from the exercise so that they are true for them – but still include the target vocabulary (for more on personalizing, see Tip 38).
- Make flexible: in teacher-led 'ping-pong' interaction, instead of going through the exercise in the set order, tell learners to read through, and raise their hands to answer any they are sure they can get right. Or if they are working in pairs, they do all the items that together they can get right and ask you or other students about the others.

> It is both conducive to learning and interesting if learners
> can review new vocabulary items by relating these to
> themselves in some way.

Personalizing means relating the vocabulary you want to review to the
individual student: experiences, preferences, opinions, personalities,
routines, occupations and so on.

A simple example: if you have a set of words and expressions from
a coursebook unit you have just studied, or a reading text, write or
display these on the board, and then invite students to choose one and
compose a sentence that relates to themselves in some way.

Other ideas:

- With the help of students, write on the board all the verbs they have
  learnt in the last few weeks. Then invite students to write sentences
  describing an experience they have had, using one or more of the
  verbs in the past; or a routine, using the present.
- Ask individual students to share words or expressions that they
  have learnt in the last few weeks that they particularly like; or find
  particularly difficult to remember; or that are meaningful to them for
  some personal reason.
- Write on the board a word or expression that you have recently
  taught and ask students to say what personal associations it
  suggests, and why.
- Brainstorm on the board words for positive personal qualities: *friendly,
  sympathetic, reliable, good-looking* … then give each student the name
  of one other student and invite them to write down on a piece of paper
  the words that they think apply to their partner, and on another the
  words that they think apply to themselves. Then invite them to share.
- Ask students to think of a profession they would love to follow (it
  can be the one they actually have, but not necessarily). Then ask
  them to make a list of all those words which are associated with this
  profession. Later, they can share the list with other members of the
  class and challenge them to identify which profession it represents.

39 Review after a time-gap

> It's tricky to decide how long to wait before reviewing vocabulary we have just taught. Immediate recall is useful as a start, but won't result in long-term retention on its own.

If learners are taught a new item, they will take it into short-term memory. We then need to run a review before they have forgotten it, so that they will be able to retrieve its form or meaning – albeit with an effort – if challenged. After this second learning, they are likely to remember it a bit longer so we can allow a longer gap before reviewing again … and so on, until the item is probably firmly established in their memory. This is the principle called *expanding rehearsal*: allowing longer and longer gaps between reviews in order to make sure that something is permanently remembered.

In practice, this means running the first review at the end of the lesson, assuming you taught the new vocabulary at the beginning, the second some time in the succeeding lesson, then a third a week or so later, and a fourth after a month or so.

Of course, it is not reasonable to expect either materials writers or teachers to implement expanding rehearsal as consistently as this for every new vocabulary item taught. But it is a useful basic principle to remember. One problem is that coursebooks tend to provide new vocabulary in a unit, and then review it at the end of the unit, or in parallel workbooks or online practice material – and then move on to the next unit and never look at the previously-taught vocabulary again. It's up to you to make sure that you provide opportunities later in the term or year for your students to do periodic **retrieval**-based vocabulary review activities (see Tip 36) on items taught in previous units. One strategy that can help here is what is called *narrow reading*: introducing further reading texts later that deal with the same topic as earlier ones, and which are therefore likely to provide further exposure to the relevant vocabulary.

Try to avoid word games

> Word games like the one still popularly known as
> 'Hangman' are used by teachers in many classrooms: they
> are fun, but they don't teach much.

'Hangman' is a game where the teacher writes a series of dashes on the board, each representing one of the letters of a word, and challenges the students to call out letters they think are in it. If they call out a letter that is in the word, the teacher writes it in; if it is not, he or she adds a component of a sketch of a 'hanging man': the goal is to guess the word before the teacher completes the picture. Nowadays, we try to avoid the title 'hangman' and the hanging man drawing (see the reference below).

The goal of this game is usually described as 'in order to review (the spelling of) a word'. But most of the time is spent calling out names of letters until there are enough filled in to be able to identify the actual word – which happens only during the last few seconds of the game. For only these few seconds are the learners actually engaging with the target item.

The same goes for 'wordsearch', where the learners search for single words hidden in a square of criss-crossed words: if you watch what they are doing, the students are normally spending much more time on searching-but-not-finding than they are on searching-and-finding.

In addition, such word games are limited to single words, out of context, without any requirement to understand meanings in order to succeed. The teacher can, of course, add these factors by the use of additional tasks or information, but they are not an essential component of the basic game.

Such activities are useful as 'fillers' and popular with students, so use them occasionally if you have extra time on your hands at the end of a lesson, or to calm down a noisy class, or if you and the students need to take a break from intensive learning tasks. But don't make them a staple component of vocabulary review: as far as learning outcomes are concerned, they are mostly a waste of time.

Ur, P. (2012). *Vocabulary Activities* (page 233). Cambridge: Cambridge University Press.

41 Use collaborative activities

Collaborative activities are ones where learners work together to get better results than they could have done on their own, and where there are opportunities for peer-teaching.

Collaboration is not, in my view, a value in itself: you should not ask students to work together just for the sake of the collaboration – only if it is clear that such work will be beneficial to all participants. If you ask learners to write a sentence in collaboration using a new word, for example, it is very likely that one of them will do all the work and the others will be relatively inactive; in such a case you will get far more participation – and learning – if they work individually.

'Information gap' tasks – where one participant needs to convey information to another – clearly have to be done in pairs or groups. Other than these, the main types of tasks appropriate for collaborative work are those where the task is based either on recall or on gathering ideas (brainstorming, for example). A larger number of participants will always recall or think of more ideas than will a single individual. So tasks like 'see how much of the vocabulary we learnt last week you can remember' – are best done collaboratively.

A useful sequence is to ask students to do a vocabulary task on their own, and then join with other students to add to, or improve or correct it (see an example in Tip 58).

Note that collaboration does not necessitate pair or group work. It is also involved in procedures like 'Pass it round', where vocabulary-based worksheets move from one student to another to be added to or changed (see Tip 60), or 'mingling', where students meet partners briefly to exchange ideas and then move on to meet someone else (see Tip 61), or even full-class pooling of ideas or 'brainstorming' (see Tip 64).

Encourage learners to use new vocabulary in their own speech and writing

> The majority of vocabulary review activities in our materials invite learners to identify or understand the new items; very few actually get them to produce them in their own output.

It is rather difficult to design activities that get learners to use newly-learnt items productively. You can give an **L1** equivalent, or a definition, or a context with a gap left for the target item, and hope that the students will produce the word or phrase you are aiming for, but they may suggest something else. It is not surprising, therefore, that most vocabulary exercises in our textbooks or, indeed, online, present the learner with the target item and then require them to do something with it: match with another, or insert in a sentence, or determine if a sentence including it is true or false – which all involve only **receptive knowledge**. It is, however, important also to find ways of getting the learners to produce the vocabulary themselves.

One way of doing this is to give tasks that explicitly require inclusion of vocabulary learners have studied in a spoken or written assignment. If a set of new words and phrases has been learnt through a text, then they can be asked to do assignments based on that text that will naturally provide a context for use of the new items. They can be asked, for example, to use at least seven (or however many you think appropriate) vocabulary items from the original text in a summary of its content; or in a rewriting of the text in a different format or different genre (as a slide presentation, as an email, as a conversation), or in a critique of its ideas.

If the vocabulary you want students to produce is not from a particular text, then simply ask them to try to compose a story that includes as many of the items as possible: an entertaining exercise that can be done orally in small groups.

F: Teaching vocabulary from a reading text

Perhaps the most common source of new vocabulary in the language classroom is the reading text. It is therefore worth thinking carefully about how to choose which items from a text to focus on, and how.

---

43 Be selective in deciding which vocabulary to teach

44 Use vocabulary profilers

45 Check if there are useful multi-word items in the text

46 Draw attention to vocabulary learners have been taught before

47 Encourage learners to choose which vocabulary to learn

48 Pre-teach some of the new vocabulary, sometimes

49 Be wary of asking learners to infer meanings from context

Be selective in deciding which vocabulary to teach

> A major function of coursebook reading texts is to be a source of new language to be learnt. A lot of their vocabulary is, therefore, likely to be unknown to learners. We can't expect them to remember it all, and need to prioritise.

A new reading text is often, at first encounter, mostly incomprehensible to learners: a large proportion of the important content words are likely to be unknown. They will have to understand these in order to understand the text. So we will probably need to clarify the meanings of most of them: either in advance (see Tip 48) or in the course of the reading. Your coursebook may provide a list of items to be learnt; but it is better to go through the text yourself in advance and note down all the vocabulary that you are fairly sure that most of your students will not know.

Some of the items listed will be ones that are relatively rare: relevant to this particular topic, but not widely used outside it. For example, a text on Socrates might include the word *hemlock*. You would need to explain that it is a type of poison, in order for the students to understand the text; but it is not necessary for them to write it down, review it or be tested on it, since they are unlikely to encounter it elsewhere or need it for their own output.

When making a list of vocabulary to be taught from a text, it is important to note those you think may be useful for students' own future communicative purposes – ones which occur relatively commonly in the language – and make sure that these are written down and reviewed later. Rarer ones, or ones whose use is confined to very specific contexts, can be clarified temporarily to enable the students to understand the text, but do not need to receive much further attention.

44   **Use vocabulary profilers**

> A very useful tool that has been developed based on corpus analysis is the vocabulary profiler, which analyses a text and tells you how common a particular word is.

In teaching vocabulary from a reading text, we clearly need to prioritise items that are likely to be most useful to our students (see Tip 43). It is useful to employ online vocabulary **profilers** which can scan a text and provide information on the frequency of its vocabulary.

Some useful profilers are:

For English: *Text Inspector*: http://englishprofile.org/wordlists/text-inspector

Word and phrase: https://www.wordandphrase.info/academic/analyzeText.asp

For English or French: *Lextutor*: https://www.lextutor.ca/vp/comp/

For German, French or Spanish: *Multilingprofiler*: Multilingprofiler.net

The frequency may be defined according to **CEFR** levels (A1, A2, etc.), or through specifying in which thousand words it occurs in a frequency list: whether it is in the top most common thousand words ('K1') or the second ('K2'), and so on.

The results of a profiler analysis can be very helpful in choosing which vocabulary to prioritise, but you will also need to use your own professional judgement in interpreting and using them (see also Tip 8). For example, profilers usually define a word's level according to its most common meaning, but your text may be using it in a less common one; or the programme cannot identify **multi-word items,** and therefore relates to each word separately. The databases (corpora) on which the profilers are based will also make a difference: for example, how much of the **corpus** is based on written or spoken text.

Check if there are useful multi-word items in the text

> We naturally look out for new words to teach in a text, and it's easy to miss the multi-word items, which are no less important.

When preparing a text, it's a good idea to check through for new vocabulary that will need teaching (see Tip 43). Having done this, go through again, and see if you have missed any groups of words that are vocabulary items in their own right (**multi-word items**, see Tip 4). For example, in the introductory sentence above, the phrase *look out for* is, as are all phrasal verbs, a multi-word item, whose meaning is different from *look*, and different also from *look for* or *look out*. Multi-word items are very easy to miss, and coursebooks which provide lists of vocabulary to learn from a text commonly neglect them.

If we ask students to list vocabulary they don't know in a text, they will typically list single words, and probably will not be able on their own to identify unknown multi-word items. This is often because such items are composed of single words which they do know, or think they know – as in the example above. We therefore cannot rely on students to identify new multi-word items, and need to do so for them. Most important to teach, of course, are those which are *non-compositional*: the meaning of the item could not easily be guessed by knowing the meanings of each of the component words (like *by and large*, for example).

I have made the point elsewhere (see Tip 16) that when introducing a new word it is good to teach which other words it tends to go (**collocate**) with. The reading text is an opportunity to see such links in context. Where two collocated words occur next to each other, and the combination is frequently used, they become multi-word items in their own right, and it is useful to draw students' attention to them: for example, *wrong* collocates more often with *completely* than with *absolutely* or *definitely*, so the phrase *completely wrong* is worth teaching.

46 Draw attention to vocabulary learners have been taught before

> It is important to teach the new vocabulary in a text: but it is no less important to draw students' attention to those items they have been taught before but may not remember.

All classes are mixed-level: some students will be more knowledgeable or fluent in the **target language** than others. There is always new vocabulary that you are fairly sure most students will not know, and that will need teaching; but there are also items that yes, you have already taught, but that some students may not remember. So when you are considering which vocabulary needs teaching, note items like these that you'd like to remind the students about.

If you use a vocabulary **profiler** (see Tip 44), you will be looking for words that the profiler tells you are at or above your students' target level as indicated by their frequency; but look also at the words that the program indicates are one level lower. You may find that many of these are worth a reminder – or even, for some students, teaching as new items.

It is not a waste of time to ask students about a particular word and then find out that most of them remember or can easily work out what it means: on the contrary, it is a useful added review, and very helpful to those who didn't remember it, or weren't sure.

There are also 'middle-ground' words: ones which are partly new, partly known: perhaps in the present context new in either form or meaning, but clearly connected to ones already taught. These include words which look the same but are here used in a different **part of speech** (if, for example, students have learnt *impact* as a noun and come across it here as a verb *to impact*) or even with a completely different meaning (*board* in the classroom versus *board* as a kind of committee). There are also those which are clearly from the same **word family** as a word already taught, and can be linked to it (*beauty*, when they have already learnt *beautiful*).

Encourage learners to choose which vocabulary to learn

> Having noted which vocabulary in a text is, in your view, most important to teach, it is good also to allow students some choice of which items they want to learn.

On a first encounter with a text, it is certainly useful to clarify meanings of any new vocabulary, and then ask learners to note down the items that are most important (see Tip 43). But of course some learners already know more than others, and some may be interested in learning items that others are not. So it's good to allow some latitude for choice.

Students first need to notice items they didn't know before. Conventionally, this is done by asking them to underline (or highlight) words they didn't know before in a text. A less conventional, but perhaps more learner-friendly strategy, is to ask them to underline everything they *do* know: it's encouraging to realise how much of a text they already understand.

Then, when you have been through the text once and clarified items, ask each student to note down those items that he or she feels are important to remember. They might share and compare their lists at this point: to explain why they find particular items important, or why others are less so, and to help each other if there are any meanings they are not quite sure about.

After this process, you may want to ensure that the essential items you have prioritised (see Tip 43) are on everybody's list (if not already known). But beyond this, there will be individual differences in which items different students want to learn. This helps to cater for mixed levels – less advanced students will list fewer, or more basic, items; the more advanced will list more, or more difficult ones. It also helps students to feel a sense of ownership of the items they have chosen.

48 Pre-teach some of the new vocabulary, sometimes

> Pre-teaching vocabulary is, in many classrooms, a regular preliminary routine before teaching a reading text. Sometimes, however, it may be better to wait and teach the new items as they come up in the text.

A problem with pre-teaching vocabulary is that one teaching of a new item does not result in permanent learning: in fact, learners tend to forget new items fairly quickly unless they are reviewed (see Tip 34). So if you have taught the new item at the beginning of the lesson and then encounter it within the text 20 minutes later, the learner may not remember what it means. And the more items you have taught, the more overload on the learners' memory, and the fewer they are likely to remember.

If you pre-teach, therefore, it is best to limit the number of items: choose the ones that are most essential for understanding the text. And introduce them in a previous lesson, giving students time to review them both at the end of that lesson and again at the beginning of the next one.

It is, however, perfectly legitimate not to pre-teach the new vocabulary at all, but to launch straight into the text, with perhaps some preliminary discussion of the topic. You can then help students to understand the new vocabulary in the course of teaching the text. This way, the new item is taught in context, and the teaching of meaning is reinforced by the content of the surrounding text; the students also see how it links with other words in the sentence. If it is an important item for students to learn, you can pause to write it on the board, and then allow more time later for them to write it down and review it.

Whether or not you pre-teach vocabulary, it is important to list and review later those items which you feel it is particularly important for students to remember.

Be wary of asking learners to infer meanings from context

A popular procedure when teaching a reading text to intermediate or advanced learners is to ask them to infer the meaning of a new word from context. This may not be a good idea.

The main reason why inferring meaning from context (**inferencing**) is not very useful is that evidence indicates that learners are likely to guess wrong (see the reference below). This is not just because they don't understand all the words of the surrounding text. It is mainly because in most cases the information from the surrounding text, even if the reader understands all of it, does not provide sufficient clues to the meaning of the unknown word.

This does not mean we should never ask our students to guess meanings from context, or that we shouldn't suggest strategies that will help them to do so. Inferencing is a useful tool for reading, particularly when a student does not have any other source available to tell them the meaning of an unknown word. Even if the exact meaning of the word is not clear, often a rough idea of 'the kind of thing' is sufficient for reading comprehension.

For the purposes of vocabulary learning, however, a rough idea of 'the kind of thing' is inadequate: we want our students to know what the word means. If there is an unknown word in a text, therefore, it is probably not a good idea to ask them to guess its meaning, unless we are sure there are sufficient comprehensible clues in the surrounding text to enable them to guess correctly. In most cases, a request to inference the meaning of a new word will take time and is likely to result in wrong guesses. It is probably better simply to tell learners what it means, and then use the time saved to engage with the new word in context.

Nassaji, H. (2003). 'L2 vocabulary learning from context: Strategies, knowledge sources and their relationship with success in L2 lexical inferencing.' *TESOL Quarterly,* 37(4), 645–670.

G: Vocabulary enrichment and expansion

Most of our students' vocabulary learning will be based on encounters with new items learnt in the course of reading or hearing texts or doing communicative tasks; but this is not enough. We also need occasionally to initiate focused procedures whose goal is to broaden or deepen vocabulary knowledge.

> New vocabulary does not always have to be learnt in context. There's a place for initiating teaching of new words or phrases simply for the sake of expanding learners' knowledge: the contextualisation can come later.

Vocabulary expansion activities of the kind I am suggesting here are not usually very long – a few minutes at most. So they can be integrated into a lesson as a break, or bridge, between longer reading or communicative tasks; or used to introduce or round off a lesson.

Some examples:

- 'Sun-ray' brainstorms: write a theme in the middle of the board, and invite students to suggest all the words or phrases they can think of that relate to it. Write up their suggestions around the central theme, joining these to it by radiating lines. Add contributions of your own: items that they didn't know before but you would like them to learn.
- 'Sun-ray' **collocations**: as above, but the items the students are invited to contribute are all the words they can think of that would 'go with' the central word in a phrase. And then you add ones they hadn't known before. For example, you might write a noun (e.g., *question*), and invite them to think of all the adjectives that go with it (*easy, odd, funny* …); or vice versa. Or verbs that could go with an adverb, or vice versa.
- Word families: write a word on the board, and invite students to add any others from the same **word family**: for example, if you write up *hand* they might suggest *handle* (n), and you can add *handle* (v), *to hand … to, to hand over, handy, a handful.*
- Words we want to know: invite students to write down words in their own language that they would like to know how to say in the **target language**. Then invite some of the students to share, and tell them the translations; carry on with the others in a later lesson.

See the next few tips for some more activities aimed at expanding or deepening vocabulary.

> Interestingly, the most significant increase in English
> vocabulary listed in the Oxford English Dictionary each
> year is not new words but new meanings for old words.

Most common words in the language have more than one meaning.
Mainly, these added meanings are obvious metaphorical extensions –
like the head on a body coming to mean the head (director, principal,
boss) of an organisation in English. This is called *polysemy*. In the
learners' mother tongue, the metaphorical meaning may or may not
be the same: in many cases it is not, and the use of the word in its
new sense needs teaching. Or the students may already know the
metaphorical meaning and you may wish to teach the previous, but
perhaps less used, more concrete meaning: for example, they may know
dear as used to express affection, but may not know its original, but less
common, meaning of 'expensive'.

In other cases, the word the learners have already learnt may be
identical in spelling and/or pronunciation to another totally different
word – a *homonym* – which will typically appear as a separate entry
in a dictionary: like, for example, *date* (day in a calendar) and *date* (a
fruit). Homonyms will normally be taught as separate words as they
come up; there is no point in teaching *date* the fruit linked to *date* the
day in the calendar.

When the new meaning is based on polysemy, however, it can be helpful
to teach new senses of previously-learnt words, since there will usually
be an association between the meanings of the new and the old which
will help students remember the new one.

You can teach new meanings by simply writing up a known word on
the board and teaching two or three of its other meanings; or when
a new meaning for an old word comes up in a text, draw students'
attention to it, and possibly add more. Or send them to look up the
word in a dictionary (see Tip 53).

It's a good idea to have a routine slot in your lesson for teaching new vocabulary, not necessarily connected to other parts of the lesson. A neat way of doing this is 'Word of the day'.

In 'Word of the day' you simply teach a new item, for its own sake. It may indeed be a new word, but it may also be a phrase, **idiom**, quotation or proverb – or anything which you feel is useful vocabulary enrichment and likely to interest the students. The procedure takes not more than a minute or two and can be used as a routine opening to a lesson. Alternatively, it can be introduced between longer language-focused or communicative procedures in order to give students a short break or add variation.

The item may be associated with a theme you are currently discussing in class, or with something in the news; or it can be totally out of the blue. Write it up on the board and teach it as you would teach any other item (see the suggestions in Section C), adding a couple of sample contexts of use.

Another way of running 'Word of the day' is to hand responsibility over to the students. Tell them to find out for homework an interesting new word or phrase (or idiom, quotation or proverb) in the **target language** that they are fairly sure the other members of the class don't know yet, and come to class to teach it. Then each lesson a different member of the class presents their item to the rest of the class. (But make sure, if you do it this way, that you have a reserve 'Word of the day' yourself, in case the student is not prepared!)

Finally, whether the new items come from you or from the students, make sure you write them down and review them later, as you would with any other vocabulary you are teaching in class.

53 Use dictionaries and thesauri for vocabulary expansion

A dictionary is normally used for finding out the meaning of a given word; and a thesaurus, or detailed dictionary of synonyms and opposites, for finding words that express a given meaning. But they can be used also for vocabulary expansion.

When we send students to the dictionary, it is usually in order to look up a word whose meaning they do not yet know. In this case, however, we suggest they go to a dictionary – monolingual or bilingual – to look up a word they **do** already know, in order to find out more about it. Tell students: 'You have five minutes: look up this word in the dictionary, and find something about it you didn't know before.'

The dictionary can not only provide other meanings that the students did not know before (see Tip 75), but also whole expressions that include the target item, and often other words from the same **word family** that are listed in the same entry. Some dictionaries will also give added interesting information: how frequent the word is; whether it is formal or informal (see Tip 31); whether it has a particular **connotation** (see Tip 32).

A similar exercise can be done with a thesaurus. 'What other words or phrases are there that express the same sort of thing as X? Find as many as you can in five minutes.' Or 'What words or phrases are there that express the opposite of Y?' Or 'What adjectives are there that express ideas close to the meaning of the noun Z?'

These tasks can be done either in class or for homework. In either case it's useful to do a 'sharing' follow-up when you can comment on some or all of their findings.

It's probably easiest to use online resources for this activity, so you will need to provide students in advance with links that will take them to the dictionary or thesaurus you have chosen.

Teach prefixes and suffixes selectively

It is often assumed that it is useful to teach prefixes and suffixes in order to help students enrich their vocabulary. This may not always be true: it depends on the level of the students and on the affix to be taught.

It is, of course, essential to teach **affixes** (**prefixes** and **suffixes**) that indicate grammar: the *-ed* ending to indicate a past tense in English, for example. (In English, these are all suffixes, but in other languages there may also be grammatical prefixes.)

Derivational affixes – like *pre-* meaning 'before', or *-ment* indicating that the word is a noun in English – are less essential, at least for lower-intermediate (B1) students. Many teachers assume that if a learner knows the **base word** and also knows the affix, they can put these together in order to understand a new derived word. The problem is that this is simply not true for the majority of words in English at B1 level because the affix is attached to a base word that is incomprehensible to learners (*prefer*, for example), or because the total meaning of the word is not the same as we would expect by combining the meanings of its components (*interview*), or because a learner will have learnt the derived word earlier anyway, so knowing the affix won't help (*beautiful*).

I checked out this issue by searching through corpus-based frequency lists, and found that the only affixes likely to help learners at this level with new words were the suffixes *-ly* (indicating an adverb) and *-er* indicating a person engaged in a particular profession or activity.

At higher levels, however, it may be worth teaching a variety of derivational affixes. By this time learners are likely to already know a number of derived words that use a particular affix (*-ism*, for example), and raising awareness of the meaning of the affix may help them understand new words they come across that use it.

Ur, P. (forthcoming). 'How useful is it to teach affixes in intermediate classes?'

Explore synonyms

A useful way to deepen, rather than broaden, learners' vocabulary knowledge is to explore the meanings or uses of two or more words that mean 'the same sort of thing' (synonyms).

This exercise starts with the presentation of two or more **synonyms** the students already know. You might, for example, suggest *kid* and *child* in English. Identify first the basic meaning that they have in common, and then challenge the students to suggest ways in which they are different. If they don't know, then teach them. (In this case, the difference is one of formality level: *kid* is normally used in informal conversation, *child* in more formal contexts.)

There are many other distinctions that can be clarified through a study of synonyms. Here are some possibilities:

- details of denotation (*seat / chair*)
- gender-specific versus non-gender-specific (*policeman / police officer*)
- mainly concrete versus mainly abstract (*large / great*)
- different **collocations** (*tall + person / high + mountain*)
- different **connotations** (*damp / moist*)
- direct v euphemistic (*died / passed away*)

Often, of course, you may find more than one distinction: the connotations of a word, for example, are likely to determine, or be closely linked to, its possible collocations.

The exercise becomes more revealing and more complex the higher the level. For example, what are the similarities and differences between *creature* and *animal*? And working on a whole group of words with similar meanings can be even more challenging – and interesting (for example, *quarrel / fight / feud / argument / war*).

You can find synonyms to work on in a dictionary of synonyms or a thesaurus; alternatively, give a 'starter' word to students and challenge them to find one or more words that mean more or less the same.

Compare target language words or phrases with their L1 translations

If you know your students' mother tongue, then a good way of deepening and refining learners' awareness of the meanings and uses of target-language vocabulary items is to compare and contrast them with L1 equivalents.

Translating a word or phrase to or from **L1** can often illuminate aspects of the meaning of the target-language item. An obvious example of this is the phenomenon of **false friends**, where a word in the **target language** sounds – and sometimes is spelt – similarly to one in the L1, but actually has a different meaning (such as *actual* in English compared to similar-sounding words in French, Spanish or German).

Other differences may be less easily identified, but working on translation can help students become aware of them. Here are some examples:

- Choose a word that you know could translate into various different equivalents in the L1. How many translations can the students find?
- Consider a target-language **multi-word item** (like *of course* or *take care of* in English, see Tip 4). Is it also a multi-word item in the L1, or a single word? Or both?
- Look at collocational links in the target language such as *take + a decision* in English or *work + hard*. In the L1 do we also 'take' a decision? Do we work 'hard'? Or will the **collocation** be different?
- Consider a target-language word or phrase and its most obvious translation into L1. Are there any differences in meaning? In the kinds of context it appears in? In collocational links?
- Invite students to translate entire sentences from a reading text into their L1. Where are the differences of opinion as to the best translation? What does this reveal about the meaning or use of the vocabulary of the original text?
- Invite students to do the reverse: translate a sentence or newspaper heading from L1 into the target language, and again explore issues of meaning or use that arise.

H: Activities and materials for vocabulary review and expansion

This section presents a set of basic types of activities or materials, with variations, which can be exploited in order to review or enrich learners' vocabulary in ways that are interesting and learning-rich. They also give some scope for the students to function at different levels and speeds.

Dictation is frowned upon by some as being too
mechanical and boring: but it can be used in different ways
and is a useful way of providing quick vocabulary review.

If students write down words dictated by the teacher, then they are
essentially retrieving the written form of a word in response to its spoken
form. The aspect of meaning is less focused on. It is, however, extremely
difficult to write down a word from dictation if you don't understand
it. (Get someone to dictate you a few words in a language unfamiliar to
you, and you'll see what I mean!) Learners who successfully complete a
dictation are likely, therefore, to have understood what they have written.

There are variations on the dictation procedure which can make it more
meaningful and perhaps more interesting for learners. Here are some
possibilities:

- **Chunk** translation: dictate brief phrases or full sentences.
- Reading-dictation: dictate a word or phrase from a reading text and
  ask the students to find and underline the relevant portion of text.
- Translation-dictation: dictate the word or phrase in **L1** and ask
  students to write the target-language translation, or vice versa.
- Completion-dictation: dictate a beginning of a sentence that includes
  the target word or phrase; students write it down, and then complete
  the sentence any way they like.
- Speed-writing dictation: read out a set of words or phrases at
  normal speed. Students write down as many as they have time for.
  Optionally, add a second reading, where they can add more.
- Dicto-gloss: read aloud a text of about 100 words to students at
  normal speaking speed while they make notes of the content. They
  then come together in pairs or groups to try to reconstruct as much
  of the text as they can remember, based on their notes. Optionally,
  write on the board the main words or phrases that you want them
  to include in their reconstruction; and/or read the text to them
  again after they have worked for a few minutes. Finally, display or
  distribute the original written text for checking.

58 Challenge learners to recall

Asking learners to recall from memory items that they have previously been taught is a quick and effective way to reinforce learning.

After having taught some vocabulary at the beginning of a lesson, we will need to review it later, or at the end of the same lesson. We could just re-teach the items, or draw students' attention to them if we have written them on the board, but it is far more helpful to ask students to close their eyes and see how many of the new items they can recall on their own, before reminding them of any they have forgotten. Successful recall in itself reinforces learning much better than just being reminded (see Tip 36).

Later review can also be based on recalling activities. A favourite of mine is 'Recall and share'. Write or display 10 to 15 new vocabulary items on the board, and tell students to study them for a few seconds and try to memorise them all, without writing them down. Then hide or delete the items, and give students a few seconds to try to write down as many as they remember. When they have written as many as they can, tell them to share with other class members sitting near them, and see if together they can recall more – or all of them. At this point they can also help each other with spelling. Finally, re-display the items on the board for self-check, and make sure that the meanings of all the items are known.

Another variation is recalling whole phrases or sentences. For example: after completing a conventional vocabulary exercise, tell students to close their books and try to recall any of the sentences that were in the exercise – or even just phrases from them that included the target items. Similarly, after doing a reading text, write on the board a selection of the items you wanted the students to learn from it, and challenge them to recall – without peeping! – the phrases in which these items occurred.

> A useful procedure for reviewing new vocabulary
> is to challenge students to compose sentences that
> contextualise them.

Such procedures can, however, become rather tedious. Here are a few
ways of varying them:

- Compose a *negative* sentence that includes any one of the items.
- Compose a *question* that includes any one of the items.
- Compose a sentence that includes any *two* of the items.
- Compose a sentence including one of the items, that is a *false* statement.
- Compose a sentence including one of the items that expresses a *true fact about yourself*.
- Compose *an entire story* that includes as many of the items as you can.

The first five of these can be run as an informal full-class interaction, with
students calling out their ideas as they think about them. Alternatively,
they can be done in writing, either in class or for homework, with sharing
of ideas – in full class, or in groups – as an optional follow-up. I prefer
to run the last procedure as informal oral work in groups, without any
writing at all: the students in the group take turns to add 'episodes' to a
story, each including at least one of the target items. You may or may not
want to ask groups to report their stories afterwards.

The tasks listed above are more interesting than the conventional 'compose
a sentence' for two main reasons. First, most of them require some form of
higher-order thinking skills: thinking about connections between concepts,
for example, or evaluating truth and falsehood, or creative processes in the
story composition. Second, there is personalization – connecting the item
to learners' own experience, opinions etc. – required explicitly in the fifth
task above, but very often appearing also in responses to the others.

Finally, note that when we talk about 'contextualising' a vocabulary
item, the context in question does not necessarily need to be a full
sentence. It's fine to ask students to suggest two-, three- or four-word
phrases that make sense and include the target vocabulary.

'Pass it round' is a procedure in which learners collaborate by adding ideas to worksheets that other learners have already written on.

This is best explained by an example. Choose a set of 20 or 30 words you have taught that have fairly clear opposites. Prepare copies of worksheets with these words written in a 'scatter', each one with a space after it to write in an opposite. Distribute the worksheets to students and ask each to write in any four opposites they can think of in the spaces provided. When they have written four, they raise the worksheet above their heads, and exchange it with another student who has finished and raised the worksheet. They write another four opposites, and then swap again, until at least one of the worksheets is finished. Then display a copy of the filled-in worksheet for checking.

Doing it this way is better than just 'pass to your neighbour' which tends to produce 'bottlenecks' and is uncomfortable for students who work more slowly and feel they are holding up the others, or for faster ones who are hanging around waiting. An alternative solution to this problem is to limit by time rather than number of items: tell students to write in as many words as they can until you stop them; then they exchange worksheets with a neighbour.

Either way, this procedure ensures that all the students are engaging with target items all the time, with no pressure to work faster or slower than their natural speed. There is also a pleasant feeling of collaboration (see Tip 41).

Other variations:

- Ask students to add another word which could go (**collocate**) with the given word;
- Ask students to translate;
- Give only a single (different) theme word or phrase in the centre of each page: each student adds as many associations as he or she can think of and then passes it on to someone else to add more.

Mingling is a classroom procedure where learners move around the classroom space, meeting and exchanging information with others.

Like 'Pass it round', mingling ensures that all the learners are engaged in a vocabulary learning activity all the time, instead of hanging around waiting for a single student nominated by the teacher to answer a question. It also causes them to get up and move around, which can be a welcome break from the static nature of most classroom procedures.

For example: invite each student to choose a word or phrase that they think some or all of the other students may not know (they can be asked to prepare this for homework). Tell them to write the word on a piece of paper. Alternatively, you prepare slips of paper to distribute with new words or phrases you want students to learn, together with their explanations and/or translations. The slips could also contain target-language proverbs or famous quotations or useful **idioms**. At first, students simply join whoever is sitting near them and explain their vocabulary item to each other (it doesn't matter too much if the other student already knows it). They then exchange their papers and look around for another student to explain their new item to and swap with. Sooner or later they will need to stand up, move around, and find students who were not sitting near them to exchange papers with.

A similar procedure can be used to engage with other kinds of vocabulary-linked activities:

- Each student chooses a word he or she has found particularly difficult to remember; or a favourite word; or a funny word. They then mingle in order to share and exchange words.
- Each student chooses a strategy they have found particularly helpful in learning vocabulary in the **target language**.

In an optional follow-up session, students share vocabulary or vocabulary-learning strategies that they have learnt in the procedure and find particularly useful or interesting.

62 Use word cards

> Word cards are pieces of paper or card with a new vocabulary item on one side, and a translation or picture on the other. These can be large – designed to be used for display by the teacher – or small – to be used by learners in individual or group work.

Of course, these days word cards can be designed online, and projected on a screen; and online tools such as *Quizlet* are based on these. There are, however, advantages to actual paper-based cards: they can be more easily exchanged, moved around the class, fixed to a noticeboard as a permanent display, played with. The disadvantages are that they take more time to prepare and then need storage space: so only make them if you feel you will use them enough to make the investment worthwhile.

Word cards can be used, first, to teach new items: they draw attention better than just writing on the board, and can be moved forwards and backwards and around, to make sure that all students see them.

Second, they can be used for review. If the teacher keeps the cards in a box on his or her desk, then they are readily accessible for review activities such as:

- The teacher sticks the cards to the board displaying only the translation or picture; students are invited to come to the board, say what the target item is for any card, and turn it around to check.
- Students sit in groups with a pile of cards in the middle, with the translations or pictures facing upwards. They take turns to look at the top card. If the student whose turn it is can identify the target item, they get the card. If not, the card goes to the bottom of the pile.
- As students enter the classroom, they take a few of the cards and test themselves, in pairs or individually: can they identify what is on the other side of the card? They continue until the teacher begins the lesson.

Translation as a component of vocabulary – or, indeed, grammar – practice is very unfashionable today in language teaching. And yet it can make a useful contribution to learning.

I am not, of course, suggesting that translation tasks be used in preference to other kinds of exercise types, but rather that they should be added as one of a varied repertoire of vocabulary-practice activities.

Requiring students to provide an **L1** equivalent to a target item is an easy way to get them to retrieve the meaning of a word if they are given the form; and doing the same the other way round gets them to retrieve a form in response to a given meaning. It is at the basis of many word-card review activities (see Tip 62), and of online tools such as *Quizlet*.

Such activities are not only quick and require little preparation; they also represent an underlying natural process typical of learners acquiring a new language through a systematic course of study. Most such learners (myself included) like to check their understanding of the meaning of a new item by making sure they know how it would be expressed in their own language; and it makes sense to utilise such knowledge for purposes of review.

The tasks suggested above relate to single items out of context: but there is value also in translating vocabulary items in context, phrases or full sentences, either to or from the mother tongue. The advantage of this is not only that we are reviewing words in context rather than as isolated items, but also providing opportunities to draw students' attention to how they differ from the equivalents in their mother tongue in the way they **collocate** with other words, or behave grammatically. This kind of contrastive awareness can help students avoid errors when using the new vocabulary in their own production.

64 Use open-ended tasks (questions with lots of right answers)

Conventional coursebook and online vocabulary exercises are typically composed of questions that have one right answer each. But open-ended questions (ones that have lots of right answers) can be more learning rich and more interesting to do.

There are various reasons why closed-ended questions are the basis of the design of most vocabulary-review materials: because that's what we are used to; because one right answer is easier to check; because such questions are clear, simple and undemanding in terms of thinking skills. On the other hand, they are limited in the amount of review they actually provide and they tend to be boring – partly because the answers are predictable, with no opportunity for creative or original responses.

Here's an example of a multiple-choice question:

> It is important to eat (green / sweet / healthy / rich) food.

Clearly, this is aimed at reviewing the word *healthy*. But it only reviews it once, and only in one context; and the sentence is not very interesting. You could get a lot more review and a lot more interest by asking students 'What kinds of things could you describe as 'healthy'?' – and then requiring full phrases in answer ('healthy exercise', 'healthy food', 'a healthy lifestyle' …), or by asking them to say what they think are the characteristics of a healthy person by completing the sentence 'A healthy person …' any way they like, and then sharing ideas.

The same is true of any vocabulary item you want to review: ask students to brainstorm associations with it, or phrases that use it, or things from their own experience that relate to it. Each such question provides opportunities to review the target item several times in different contexts. The responses are also more interesting, and students are more likely to attend to them, since they are not predictable, and may be surprising, dramatic or funny.

> In *yes/no* tests the learners are given a number of
> vocabulary items they have learnt and asked to say for
> each whether or not they know them.

This procedure is usually used for testing: the idea is that you get the
students to assess their own vocabulary knowledge by responding to
each item on a worksheet (or the digital equivalent) by 'yes' (i.e. I know
this) or 'no' (I don't know it). There are clearly problems associated
with this kind of self-assessment; and in any case, I think this procedure
is far more useful as a vocabulary review than as a test.

The temptation to claim that they know more than they actually do
is obviously greater if the students are going to get a grade on their
performance: but if there is no grade, and the goal is frankly stated
as, 'Let's see how much you know, so I can remind you of any words
you've forgotten,' then it is a simple and learner-friendly way of getting
students to retrieve meanings in response to the written form of a
vocabulary item, give themselves credit if they can do so, and find out
the meanings of ones they had forgotten.

It can be made more detailed and challenging if the options are not just
'yes' or 'no' but rather '✓✓' (= I know this and could use it myself), '✓'
(= I could understand this in context, but wouldn't use it myself), '?'
(= I think I know this, but am not sure) and '✗' (= no idea!).

Clearly, this involves more preparation than most of the procedures
suggested in other tips in this section, since you need to prepare the
worksheet with the list of words that students will check through.

In a follow-up, students can join with partners in order to help
each other add 'yes' responses, before calling you in if there are any
vocabulary items neither of them can remember.

I: Testing vocabulary

It is important to test our students' vocabulary knowledge from time to time, so that both they and we are aware of how much they've learnt (or haven't) and can plan further review and teaching accordingly.

---

66 Do brief weekly quizzes
67 Include a vocabulary component in general tests
68 Include an optional component in tests
69 Test productive not just receptive knowledge
70 Get learners to design their own test items
71 Use translation for testing
72 Test (also) aspects of vocabulary other than written form and meaning

---

> It's a good idea to test learners' knowledge every week in brief quizzes, which do not take up much time, but provide valuable feedback on learning.

Regular quizzes – informal tests, done as part of the lesson with feedback provided as soon as possible – have various functions: they help both you and the students to be aware of what they have or have not successfully learnt; they function as review in themselves; and they can motivate students to re-learn the vocabulary in advance in order to ensure success. Quizzes should not be presented as formal tests – which can be stressful for some students – but frankly as a useful tool to help them (and you) to assess progress. There is, therefore, a place for self-assessment, as suggested below: there is little point in cheating if the goal is clearly ongoing feedback on learning rather than high-stakes assessment.

Make sure that the quizzes include not only vocabulary you taught last week, or recently, but also a few of those taught earlier – and that students know that these may be included. It's important to come back occasionally to review items learnt some time ago (see Tip 39).

Quizzes should be written on paper: if they are done online, then it is difficult to know if the students really knew the vocabulary, or looked it up. On the other hand, this does not necessarily mean printing out individual quiz sheets for each student: the questions can be displayed on the board, and only the answers written on paper.

You need to make sure that quizzes don't take too long: 10 to 15 minutes is plenty. The assessment of results is best done through taking in papers and checking at home: but if you have a lot of large classes, this may not be feasible. Another possibility is to display answers on the board and let students self-check; or to tell them to check in pairs and call you over if neither of the partners knows the answer.

67 Include a vocabulary component in general tests

If you have to compose formal end-of-course, or end-of-year exams in the target language as the major factor in calculating learners' grades, then it is good to include in these a section that tests vocabulary.

The main reason for this is the phenomenon of *backwash*: the effect a test has on the preceding teaching and learning. If, for example, grammar mistakes are heavily penalised in an exam, then learners will understand the need to invest time and effort into improving grammatical accuracy. Similarly, the awareness that vocabulary is explicitly tested in an upcoming exam will raise their motivation to work on expanding and deepening vocabulary knowledge.

This ought not to be so, of course: vocabulary is a major component of language proficiency in any of the four skills of listening, reading, speaking and reading, and in order to score well in tests of any of these areas, learners should be aware that they need to learn a lot of vocabulary. But it doesn't work like that. In many situations, the course is seen essentially as preparation for the exam, and if the exam components consist of reading and listening comprehension and speaking and writing tasks, then learners will expect the course content to be mostly based on these and will therefore work on them. If the exam explicitly tests vocabulary, even as a minor component, then it is more likely that they will make an effort to review vocabulary in preparation for it.

This is not to belittle the importance of the communicative skills mentioned above. Clearly, overall proficiency is primarily expressed in learners' ability to communicate in speech and writing. Any good course will teach these, and summative assessment tools – most commonly exams – will test them. My claim is only that the inclusion of an explicit vocabulary test within the exam, even as a minor component, can substantially affect the amount of time and effort learners devote to vocabulary learning, and ultimately contribute to their success in the exam as a whole.

> Normally, tests are composed of a number of sections, all of them compulsory. It is useful in your own classroom vocabulary tests to add an optional section for faster-working or more advanced learners.

When you give vocabulary tests in class, you will often have come across the phenomenon that the faster-working or more advanced students finish early, and you have to find something for them to do while the others finish – or just let them leave the room, which may disturb other students. If you add to your test an optional last section, then this solves the problem: it keeps them busy doing as much of it as they can after they have finished the rest. Also, if the test is relatively easy for the more advanced students, then this is a chance to give them something to do at a more appropriate level.

It has to be clear that they can only do the optional section if they have already finished all the rest. And in order to play fair, you need to assure all the class that if they do the rest of the test perfectly, they can still get 100 percent: the extra section may add bonus marks.

The optional part should relate to vocabulary that has not yet appeared in the previous sections and should provide students with the opportunity to show what they know. The tasks should therefore be more challenging than the conventional multiple-choice, gap-fill or matching questions that are conventionally used in vocabulary tests. Here are some ideas:

- Open sentence-completion: provide the beginnings of sentences, each one of which includes one of the items and invite students to complete as they wish;
- Invite students to list as many words as they can in the same family as each word in a given list;
- Invite students to translate into the **target language** as many as they can of a set of **L1** words or expressions;
- Invite students to write a story using a given set of vocabulary.

69   Test productive not just receptive knowledge

> Conventional vocabulary tests are based on formats that typically test only whether learners can recognise and understand the target vocabulary. We need to add ones that also test production.

Vocabulary tests consist mostly of multiple-choice questions or gap-fills to be completed from a bank of possible answers. In other words, what the test-taker has to do is identify the correct answer from those provided, rather than produce the target vocabulary themselves. This shows they have **receptive** mastery of the item – could probably understand and respond to a message that included it – but not necessarily that they could use it themselves appropriately.

The main reason for this is that test-designers need objective criteria to assess if a response is right or wrong. They therefore need a clear definition of what is a 'right' answer, so that anything else is 'wrong': and the formats described above clearly provide this. If you ask students to produce a vocabulary item you want to test – by requiring, for example, the completion of a gapped sentence that provides a context for the item, or a translation from the learner's **L1**, or a response to a **synonym** or definition – they might well produce a response which is perfectly acceptable as a response to the cue, but not actually the item you wanted to test. If you yourself are assessing them, then you will use your own professional judgement to decide if the answer is acceptable or not. But if you are looking for completely objective and reliable assessment that could be performed by a computer, then such test items are problematic.

So it's a trade-off: use only receptive items and you get objective assessment but only find out if your students can understand the vocabulary or not; use both types, and your assessment criteria will be less objective, but you will also get information on their ability to produce it. In my view, as implied in the heading to this tip, it is worth the sacrifice of complete objectivity to provide tests of **productive** as well as receptive knowledge.

Get learners to design their own test items

> It can be very useful, for a number of reasons, to get learners to design vocabulary test items for a class test, rather than doing it all yourself.

Testing is conventionally regarded as a top-down procedure: the teacher or test designer composes the test items which are seen for the first time by the students at the test event itself. This, for obvious reasons, has to be the case when the tests in question are high-stakes national or international exams. But it does not necessarily apply to classroom vocabulary tests you give at the end of a unit or even at the end of a course. In such situations it makes sense to invite students to compose some or all of the test.

Give students a list of the vocabulary to be tested, making it clear that of course not every single item will in fact appear in the final version of the test. Invite them to compose test items for as many of them as they can. This could be in class, run as individual, pair or group work, or it could be a homework assignment. A useful optional follow-up is to give time for students to share their items with one another, if they have composed items on their own, and perhaps correct each other's work if necessary. When they have finished writing, take in their suggestions and then compose the test based on some or all of them (corrected, of course, as needed), with the possible addition of further items of your own.

This way, the test is to some extent 'owned' by students and is far less scary for those who suffer from test anxiety. It also takes some of the workload off you! Finally, the composition of test items by students in itself provides extra review of the target items.

Use translation for testing

> Probably the quickest and easiest way to test if a learner
> knows the form or meaning(s) of a vocabulary item is to
> ask them to translate it to or from their L1.

Clearly this recommendation above is only feasible if the class shares
a common **L1** which the teacher also knows: but this situation is
probably true of most foreign-language classrooms in the world.

I am not suggesting that an entire written vocabulary test should be
based on translation to or from the L1. This would not only be boring,
it would also tend to mislead learners into believing that there is always
a one-to-one translation of any given vocabulary item.

However, as one of the components of a test with multiple sections, it
can be a useful addition to other types of test items. The requirement to
translate from the L1 into the **target language** has the added advantage
that it tests the learner's ability to produce, not just recognise and
understand, the vocabulary item in question. And if we challenge
learners to translate entire phrases or sentences from the L1 into the
target language, this is a good way of finding out if they can avoid
mistakes whose source is **L1 interference**: for example, if they are able
to insert an appropriate preposition following a particular adjective or
verb which takes a different preposition in their L1.

I have also found it useful as a tool to quickly assess the level of
an incoming student; I compose a list that comprises items in the
target language of different levels: starting with easy ones, getting
progressively more advanced, and embedded in longer phrases or
sentences. I then simply ask the student to translate the words into their
L1. This can be done fairly quickly in a one-to-one interview.

> Most vocabulary tests are written and therefore relate only to the written form of the items tested, and normally only to their (most common or obvious) meaning.

We do not normally test if learners can in fact recognise and/ or produce the spoken form of a vocabulary item; and we rarely test other characteristics of a word or aspects of its use in context: collocational and grammatical links (see Tips 16 and 17), register and appropriateness in context (see Tip 31).

The problem with oral tests is, of course, that they are expensive and time-consuming to run; nevertheless, it is useful, if you have time, to test if your students can in fact recognise the spoken forms (by the use of dictations, for example, see Tip 57) or produce spoken versions (get them to read aloud sentences or phrases including the target vocabulary).

One way of finding out if your students know how to use the appropriate collocational or grammatical links to target vocabulary items is to require them to actually produce sentences using them that include the problematical links: this is one of the advantages of using **L1** to L2 translation tests (see Tip 71).

Testing other aspects of meaning or use – for example, **connotation**, or appropriate contexts of use – is trickier. One possibility is to present the learner with a specific lexical item and ask them to tell you all they know about its meaning and use in context. Alternatively, there are rewriting tasks that combine grammar and vocabulary to test knowledge of appropriateness to context. For example, provide the students with a sentence that clearly belongs to informal conversation and ask them to rewrite it to make it suitable for a formal essay. Or vice versa: give a formal sentence and ask them to rewrite it in an informal style, as part of a conversation. Another similar test item could ask students to contrast a sample of texting language with its formal equivalent.

J: Encourage independent vocabulary learning

Having done all we can, as teachers, to help learners expand and consolidate their vocabulary in the target language – there comes a point where they need to take responsibility for doing so on their own. Autonomous learning, added to what they learn in our classrooms, will enable them to reach the highest levels they are capable of in vocabulary learning – and indeed in their overall level of proficiency.

Encourage out-of-class vocabulary learning

> It is essential for students to supplement learning in the classroom by looking for sources of vocabulary enrichment outside it; and the teacher can encourage out-of-class learning and suggest appropriate sources or activities.

I have several times asked English teachers who learnt English in a country where it is not normally spoken outside the classroom how they achieved their present level of proficiency: how much through lessons in school? How much through other sources outside them? Virtually nobody has said that the English lessons alone were enough. On average, the answer was 'about half and half'; a few even claimed that the majority of their learning was outside school.

If this is so, then one of our jobs as teachers is to encourage our students to look for ways of increasing their vocabulary in the **target language** from sources outside the classroom: first, by raising awareness of the need to do so (see Tip 2), and second, by setting occasional challenging vocabulary-enrichment assignments such as the following:

- Reading books or other published materials that are easy enough to be read relatively quickly (extensive reading);
- Reading websites on subjects that interest the learners;
- Preparing presentations (oral or written) on subjects that need to be researched through sources in the target language;
- Corresponding or interacting with speakers of the target language in other countries through computer-mediated communication tools;
- Watching movies in the target language without mother-tongue subtitles (but possibly with subtitles displaying the spoken text);
- Watching short YouTube clips in the target language on a variety of topics, provided they include spoken text in the target language;
- Noticing the linguistic landscape: street signs, posters, packaging texts, shop names, etc. in the target language.

In the course of any of these, learners need to be paying attention to, and making a note of, the new vocabulary they come across.

74 Teach spelling rules

This tip applies mostly to the teaching of English, which has a particularly complex spelling system; but it can be applied also to other languages.

I have mentioned in Tip 20 that it is a good idea to point out any particular features of the spelling of a new word. What I am suggesting here is devoting separate lesson time to explicit instructions in the conventions of spelling of the **target language**, reinforced by practice exercises such as dictations. These can help learners become autonomous in their writing, aided by computer spell-checks (but see below for a caveat).

Some spelling rules that it is useful to teach in English:

- The addition of an *e* after a short closed syllable (not just after single-syllable words) causes the preceding vowel to be pronounced like its name (*nine, debate*).
- Certain pairs of letters, or **bigrams**, are regularly pronounced in a certain way, which could not be predicted from the individual letters (*ee, sh, th, ch*, etc.).
- The letters *c* and *g* are normally softened to /s/ and /dʒ/ when they are followed by *e* or *i*.
- The word *all* when used as a **prefix** is shortened to *al* (*also, altogether*, not *allso, *alltogether).
- A double consonant normally ensures that the vowel preceding it will be short, as in *difficult, matter*.

Learners need to be warned that there are exceptions to these rules, particularly with very common words. For example, the *i* in *give* is pronounced /ɪ/, and the *g* preserves its 'hard' pronunciation in spite of the following *i*.

Note that use of the spellcheck feature of programs like Microsoft Word is no guarantee that the text will be free of spelling errors: paradoxically, it is the good spellers who are likely to benefit most from the use of an online spellcheck.

> Using the dictionary – whether print or digital – is not
> as easy as it might appear. Whether they are using digital
> or print dictionaries, learning some basic skills can help
> students find the meanings they are looking for more
> quickly and accurately.

I have already mentioned in Tip 24 that looking up in a dictionary is not
recommended in a teacher-led lesson. When, however, the learners are
working independently on their own reading and writing, it becomes
essential. We can help learners become effective and autonomous users of
the dictionary by suggesting and practising some basic dictionary skills.

The following suggestions are appropriate for the use of any kind of
dictionary: print or digital, monolingual or bilingual (on the latter choice,
see below). It is useful to explain strategies such as those listed below to
your students, and give opportunities in class to practise using them.

- Make a rough guess of the kind of thing the word is likely to mean
  before you look it up.
- Don't assume that the first meaning the dictionary gives is the one
  you need: look (or scroll) down and find one that makes sense in
  the context.
- Check out the expressions using the word that are given at the
  bottom of the entry: the word you are looking for may in fact be
  part of one of them.
- Look for information on any limitations on use of the word: if it
  is American or British English, if it is taboo or limited to informal
  contexts.

For learners, I am in favour of using bilingual rather than monolingual
dictionaries, even at the highest levels. The L2 explanations in a
monolingual dictionary may not be clear, and sometimes use vocabulary
that is even more difficult than the target word; **L1** translations are just
as accurate, more quickly and easily understood and a better support
for the learner working on their own.

Introduce advanced learners to phonemic symbols

> It is useful for more advanced learners to know the phonemic representations of the sounds of the language they are learning, so that even if they don't have access to the internet or a proficient speaker of the language, they can find out on their own from a print dictionary how a word is pronounced.

Until relatively recently it was standard practice in a lot of courses in English to teach learners the **phonemic** alphabet. This, however, in most cases, is no longer necessary: most digital dictionaries provide a loudspeaker icon which, if you click on it, will give you the pronunciation.

However, if learners do not have access to digital resources, and come across a new word in a text they are reading independently that they do not know how to pronounce, it is useful to be able to get this information by using the phonemic representation that appear in many good print dictionaries.

Phonemic symbols do not take too long to teach. Most (though not all) of the consonants are represented by the obvious corresponding letter: the sound of the 'n' for example is represented by /n/. The problem is mainly with the vowels, particularly in English which has far more vowel sounds than it has vowel letters: the letter 'a' could be pronounced /æ/, /eɪ/, /ɑː/ or /ɔː/ depending on the word it appears in.

You will need also to tell students how to identify the stressed syllable – normally shown by a small vertical line before the stress: for example, the word *impossible* would be represented by /ɪmˈpɒsəb(ə)l/.

It is a fun exercise to ask students to transcribe (the English, or **target language** versions of) their own names into phonemic symbols. Once you have checked these are correct, they can be copied onto a list and then students asked to identify all their classmates' names as represented phonemically.

Encourage use of online tools for vocabulary learning

> An enormous number of tools for vocabulary learning are available on the internet: these can certainly be of great help for learners who are working on improving their vocabulary on their own. The problem is choosing which to use!

Another problem is, of course, that new vocabulary websites are appearing all the time, and others are disappearing! So all I can do here is indicate a few types of sites and the names of some I have come across which appear to be likely to stay with us.

First, there are the dictionaries, thesauri and grammars, which allow learners to find out meanings, other ways of expressing similar ideas and what the correct grammatical usages are of any particular word. It is fairly easy, by inserting the target word or even an entire question into a search engine to get to the information needed.

Second, there are sites which help learners expand their vocabulary. A problem here is that most vocabulary expansion websites are based on lists of **lexical sets,** or other groups of words which are the same kind of thing, which, as we have seen (see Tip 10) is not a very good way of learning new vocabulary. Better are the ones which provide a reading text, and allow the reader to get an **L1** translation of any particular word or expression if by hovering the cursor over it. *Duolingo*, for example, does this.

Then there are the word-card sites like *Quizlet* which enable students to build up their own lists of vocabulary to learn and review, with a set of built-in testing or reviewing activities.

A useful website for more advanced explorations of vocabulary is *Lextutor* (https://www.lextutor.ca/). This resource is designed mainly as a source of information for teachers, but it also provides some useful tools for independent learners. For example, they can test themselves in order to establish what their vocabulary level is; or access a whole set of sentences that contextualise any given word.

References

Print

Boulton, A. (2017). 'Corpora in language teaching and learning.' *Language Teaching*, 50(4), 483–506.

Erten, I. H. and Tekin, M. (2008). 'Effects on vocabulary acquisition of presenting new words in semantic sets versus semantically unrelated sets.' *System*, 36(3), 407–422.

Farley, A. P., Ramonda, K. and Liu, X. (2012). 'The concreteness effect and the bilingual lexicon: The impact of visual stimuli attachment on meaning recall of abstract L2 words.' *Language Teaching Research,* 16(4), 449–466.

Karpicke, J. and Roediger, H. L. (2008). 'The critical importance of retrieval for learning.' *Science*, 319, 966–968.

Krepel, A., de Bree, E. H. and de Jong, P. F. (2021). 'Does the availability of orthography support L2 word learning?' *Reading and Writing*, 34(2), 467–496.

Laufer, B. and Rozovski-Roitblat, B. (2011). 'Incidental vocabulary acquisition: the effects of task type, word occurrence and their combination.' *Language Teaching Research*, 15(4), 391–412.

Martinez, R. and Schmitt, N. (2012). 'A phrasal expressions list.' *Applied Linguistics*, 33(3), 299–320.

Nassaji, H. (2003). 'L2 vocabulary learning from context: Strategies, knowledge sources and their relationship with success in L2 lexical inferencing.' *TESOL Quarterly*, 37(4), 645–670.

Papathanasiou, E. (2009). 'An investigation of two ways of presenting vocabulary.' *ELT Journal*, 63(4), 313–322.

Schmidt, R. W. (1990). 'The role of consciousness in second language learning.' *Applied Linguistics*, 11(2), 129–58.

Thornbury, S. (2013). The learning body. In Arnold, J. and Murphey, T. (Eds.), *Meaningful action: Earl Stevick's influence on language teaching* (pp.62–78). Cambridge: Cambridge University Press.

Tinkham, T. (1997). 'The effects of semantic and thematic clustering in the learning of second language vocabulary.' *Second Language Research* 13(2), 138–63.

Ur, P. (2012) *Vocabulary Activities*. Cambridge: Cambridge University Press

Ur, P. (forthcoming). How useful is it to teach affixes in intermediate classes?

Webb, S. (2007). 'The effects of repetition on vocabulary knowledge.' *Applied Linguistics*, 28(1), 46–65.

Online

Academic Word List (AWL) https://www.wgtn.ac.nz/lals/resources/academicwordlist/information

BNC/COCA headword list https://www.wgtn.ac.nz/lals/resources/paul-nations-resources/vocabulary-lists

Corpus of Global Web-Based English (GloWbE) https://www.english-corpora.org/glowbe/

English Vocabulary Profile (EVP) https://www.englishprofile.org/wordlists/evp

Lextutor https://www.lextutor.ca/vp/comp/

Multilingprofiler Multilingprofiler.net

New General Service List (NGSL) http://www.newgeneralservicelist.org/

Text Inspector http://englishprofile.org/wordlists/text-inspector

Word and phrase https://www.wordandphrase.info/academic/analyzeText.asp

Further recommended reading

Books

Kerr, P. (2014). *Translation and Own-language Activities*. Cambridge: Cambridge University Press.

Hinkel, E. (Ed.) (2019). *Teaching Essential Units of Language: Beyond Single-word Vocabulary*. Abingdon: Routledge.

Nation, I. S. P. (2001). *Learning Vocabulary in Another Language*. Cambridge: University Press.

Schmitt, N. (2000). *Vocabulary in Language Teaching*. Cambridge: Cambridge University Press.

Thornbury, S. (2002). *How to Teach Vocabulary*. Essex: Pearson Education Limited.

Ur, P. (2012). *Vocabulary Activities*. Cambridge: Cambridge University Press.

Research articles

Barcroft, J. (2007). 'Effects of opportunities for word retrieval during second language vocabulary learning.' *Language Learning, 57*(1), 35–56.

Laufer, B. (2005). 'Focus on form in second language vocabulary learning.' *EUROSLA Yearbook*, 5, 223–250.

Laufer, B. and Girsai, N. (2008). 'Form-focused instruction in second language vocabulary learning: A case for contrastive analysis and translation.' *Applied Linguistics*, 29(4), 694–716.

Laufer, B. and Rozovski-Roitblat, B. (2015). 'Retention of new words: Quantity of encounters, quality of task, and degree of knowledge.' *Language Teaching Research, 19*(6), 687–711.

Schmitt, N. (2008). 'Instructed second language vocabulary learning.' *Language Teaching Research*, 12(3) 329–363.

Schmitt, N. and Schmitt, D. (2014). 'A reassessment of frequency and vocabulary size in L2 vocabulary teaching.' *Language Teaching, 47*(4), 484–503.

Webb, S. (2007). 'The effects of repetition on vocabulary knowledge.' *Applied Linguistics*, 28(1), 46–65.

Glossary

Numbers in **bold** refer to the tip number(s) where the term occurs.

affix: prefix or suffix (**54**)

base word: root word, without prefixes or suffixes (**14, 54**)

bigram: two-letter combination, e.g., *ee*, *th* (**14, 20, 74**)

CEFR: The Common European Framework of Reference for Languages: a description of language proficiency levels defined from beginner to advanced as A1, A2, B1, B2, C1, C2 (**8, 13, 44**)

chunk: a vocabulary item that includes more than one word, e.g., *in any case* (**3, 4, 57**)

collocate: go with; when word A often occurs before or after word B, the two words are said to *collocate* (**16, 45, 60, 63**)

collocation: the phenomenon where a specific word tends to occur before or after another specific word; see *collocate* (**16, 50, 55, 56**)

compositional: (of a phrase) can be understood if you understand the component words, like *go up* (see **idiom**; **non-compositional**) (**4, 45**)

connotation: the underlying (usually positive or negative) messages conveyed by a word (**32, 33, 53, 55, 71**)

corpus: a large database of texts (**33, 44**)

derivational affix: a prefix or suffix that is part of the root meaning of the word (e.g., *re-*, *-ly*), as distinct from grammatical affixes (e.g., plural *-s*) (**54**)

derivative: a word made up of a **base word** together with a **derivational affix** (**5, 14**)

false friend: a word that looks like a parallel word in the learners' **L1**, but means something different (**23, 56**)

homonym: two words are homonyms if they look and sound the same, but are completely different in meaning, and from different roots (e.g., *bank: financial institution/bank: side of river*) (**51**)

idiom: a multi-word expression which is **non-compositional** and usually based on a visual image, e.g., *raining cats and dogs* (**6, 52, 61**)

inferencing: working out the meaning of a word from the context (**49**)

L1: the learners' mother tongue (**6, 11, 17, 19, 22, 23, 24, 26, 27, 28, 30, 36, 42, 56, 57, 63, 68, 69, 71, 72, 75, 77**)

L1 interference: the negative influence of the learners' mother tongue on their production in the new language (**23, 71**)

lexical set: a group of words that are all the same part of speech and mean the same sort of thing, e.g., *red*, *yellow*, *blue*, *green* (**10, 77**)

lingua franca: a language used by people to communicate with one another when they don't know each other's mother tongue (**9**)

metalanguage: the words used to describe features of language, e.g., *adjective*, *past tense* (**13**)

multi-word item: a vocabulary item that includes more than one word, e.g., *in any case* (**4, 8, 24, 29, 33, 44, 45, 56**)

non-compositional: (of a phrase) cannot be understood by combining the meanings of the component words, like *by and large* (see compositional) (**4, 45**)

part of speech: word class, the function of a word in a sentence, e.g., adjective, noun, preposition (**5, 10, 13, 22, 46**)

phonemic: relating to the sounds of a language (**76**)

phonemic transcription: the writing out of a word or phrase using phonemic symbols instead of the normal alphabet (**22**)

polyseme: a word which has more than one meaning (**15**)

prefix: an addition to the beginning of a word which changes its meaning or part of speech, e.g., *dis-*, *en-* (**5, 14, 54, 74**)

productive knowledge: thorough knowledge of a feature of the language enabling the learner to use it in his or her speech or writing (**36, 69**)

profiler: an online program based on corpus study that analyses the words in a text and tells you how common each one is (**44, 46**)

receptive knowedge: limited knowledge of a feature of the language, enabling a learner to recognise it when encountered in speech or writing, but not to produce it him- or herself (**36, 42, 69**)

retrieval: a learner's recall of the meaning or form of a new vocabulary item in response to a hint or question (**36, 39**)

semantic field: the area of meaning of a vocabulary item; e.g., *red* belongs to the semantic field of 'colours' (**10**)

suffix: an addition to the end of a word which changes its meaning or part of speech, e.g., *-ble, -ly* (**5, 14, 20, 54**)

synonym: two words are synonyms if they have similar meanings, e.g., *big/large* (**10, 26, 30, 55, 69**)

target language: the language the learners are being taught (**1, 2, 4, 6, 11, 23, 24, 26, 30, 33, 46, 50, 52, 56, 61, 67, 68, 71, 73, 74, 76**)

word family: a set of words that are derived from the same base word, e.g., *able, unable, ability, inability* (**5, 22, 46, 50, 53**)

Index